Israel in America

Israel in America

A Too-Comfortable Exile?

Jacob Neusner

Beacon Press

Boston

My thanks go to the copyright holders of the following papers for permission to reprint. The numbers preceding the titles refer to the chapters of this book. 2. "Who is Israel?" from *National Review,* 150 East 35th Street, New York City, June 24, 1977; 3. "American Jews in Israel" from *Present Tense,* Autumn 1973; 4. "Now We're All Jews — Again" from *Response,* Winter 1973–1974; 5. "The Costs of Racism for South Africa's Whites" from *Issues: The Brown Review,* February 1977; 7. "Assimilation and Self-hatred in Modern Jewish Life" from *Conservative Judaism,* Fall 1971; 8. "The Selling of Jewish Studies" from *Moment,* March 1978; 9. "Arrogance and Authenticity" from *Moment,* September 1978; 10. "Lernen and Learning" from *Journal of Reform Judaism,* Spring 1984; 12. "Faith in the Crucible of the Mind" from *America,* March 10, 1973; and 14. "Wanted: Dead or Alive" from *Moment,* January-February 1979.

Beacon Press books are published under the auspices of the Unitarian Universalist Association of Congregations in North America
25 Beacon Street, Boston, Massachusetts 02108
Published simultaneously in Canada by
Fitzhenry and Whiteside Limited, Toronto

Printed in the United States of America
(hardcover) 9 8 7 6 5 4 3 2 1

Library of Congress Cataloging in Publication Data
Neusner, Jacob, 1932–
   Israel in America.
   Includes index.
   1. Judaism — United States — Addresses, essays, lectures.
I. Title.
BM205.N485   1985   296'.0973   84–45719
ISBN 0-8070-3602-1

Contents

Preface

When Jews debate the profound issues of Jewish existence and Judaic theology, they speak of "Israel,"
meaning the Jewish people. That explains the importance, in the self-understanding of theologians, of various "Judaisms," that is, various systems composed of
a world view, a way of life, and a distinctive social group
that have, together, been characterized as Judaism.
Whether it is the reflection on the saving remnant that
constitutes Israel in the imagination of the Essene
community at Qumran, or Paul's troubled assessment
of the old Israel and the new, or the talmudic rabbis'
insistence on the sanctity and the sanctification of *all*
Israel, the subject — who is Israel — remains one and
the same. So it was David Ben-Gurion's profound understanding that led him to name the new state, formed
in the Land of Israel by the people of Israel in 1948,
the *State* of Israel.

In calling that state simply Israel, people deliver a
profound statement upon who is Israel, what is Israel,
who is the true Israel, and similar, long-vexing dilemmas
of religious thinkers in Judaism, past and present, as
well as secular Jewish thinkers today. Still, among the
many definitions of who is Israel and who is a Jew,
that of the talmudic rabbis — all Israel, born of a Jewish
mother, is Israel — remains authentic to the liturgy of
Judaism, on the one side, and its sacred srcipture, on

the other. And Ben-Gurion's daring utilization of *Israel* in an exclusive and land-centered framework challenges that liturgy and scripture. For at prayer and study, *Israel* stands for, refers to, the entire Jewish people, wherever they live: "God who keeps Israel does not slumber or sleep," is everywhere, and so watches over Israel everywhere, including Israel in the Land of Israel.

It is important to confront that peculiarity of today's language, because within it we uncover the deep issue confronting American Judaism as a religious expression and the American Jewish community as a distinct social group. That issue is whether or not Judaism and the Jews will survive, endure, and flourish in the free society of the United States of America and in other free nations like it. As I spell out matters in the opening chapter, when the large Jewish migration from the several countries of Eastern Europe — White Russia. Poland, the Ukraine, Lithuania, Romania, Slovakia and Bohemia, Hungary, and Austria — began, many reflective people thought it was the end of the Jews. "In America you cannot be a Jew, or you should not, or you do not have to." However people framed matters, the expectation remained the same. After a generation or two, it will be all over for the Jews as a distinct group — a nation-religion, an ethnic entity, however one classifies the group. The paradox is that there are, in large numbers, American Jews in the third, fourth, and fifth generations after the great migration.

There is another paradox. It is a dogma of contemporary Israeli thought that only in the State of Israel will the Jewish people endure as a nation, and Judaism (in its authentic form) continue as a viable and vital religious tradition. The *Golah,* that is, the Jews in exile from the Land of Israel, cannot for long sustain either a distinct social life or an authentic cultural and religious existence. For instance, there can be no scholarship. There can be no everyday life to express Jewish faith, on the one side, and cultural or social distinctiveness, on the other. So the judgment of European Jews who came to America and the opinion of Israeli thinkers three or four generations afterward remain the same: There can be no American Judaism, there will be no American Jews. Indeed, there should not be any.

The title of this book paradoxically defies that judgment. I maintain that there is an *Israel* in America. That is, a valid Jewish way of life, an authentic and enduring Judaic religious expression, a continuing Jewish social entity ("community," or "people," or "ethnic group"), do endure here. Exactly what it means to be Israel in America occupies the center of the chapters that follow. Written over the past fifteen years, they take up questions of both a social and a religious and sectarian character.

I begin with a picture of my view of how Judaism as we now know it took shape and how its paradoxes are to be framed and described.

I regard the critical and defining event of our age the creation of the Jewish state in the aftermath of the destruction of most of the Jews of Europe; I turn next to the issue of what it means to be a Jew, that is once

more, Israel, now in the context of this age of fulfill-
ment and realization. My focus remains on the Jews
at home. My only message to the Jews of the State of
Israel is that in 1973 they became Jews like us again.

In parts three and four, I turn to the inner life of the
American Jewish community, treating first questions
of public policy, second, issues of the imagination and
the soul. In the matter of faith, I confront, in particular, the claims and challenges of Orthodoxy. That is
not because I see the future of the American Jewish
community in the hands of Orthodox Judaism, but
because I do not, and because, like the Israelis, we
hear from the Orthodox a claim of "sole legitimacy,"
and "unique authenticity." I wish to examine that
claim and comment on it.

Finally, as I enter my fifties, I find I have a new perspective on my life and I have included a few notes
toward the autobiography I shall never write. These
are in part five. I do not think a scholar should have
an autobiography, since a scholar's books and articles
form his or her autobiography: the record of what
someone has learned and puzzled out. But I have made
some observations that concern my own life, and I
think these are worth sharing. The reason is that they
concern people other than myself. I speak for a single
segment of a whole generation of Jews, that of the
intellectuals committed to Judaism. The intellectuals
of Judaism of the third generation exercised considerable influence, because, before the community re-
formed itself, as it did, some of us thought about what
should happen and told people what we thought they

should do, along with all of us, in building Judaism in America, in the service of the part of Israel, the Jewish people, that would endure and flourish in America. We stood at the turning. The second generation looked back toward the first and could not imagine us. We look forward to the fourth and fifth, and can scarcely understand our own past. We see normality and marvel at the deep sense of abnormality of our parents. We take up the challenges of freedom, in the aftermath of destruction and despair. Our parents survived the era of anti-Semitism at home and mass murder overseas. We came to maturity in the dawn of the Jewish state in the Land of Israel and built our lives in the full light of its, and our, day.

I believe that in my work as a teacher and a scholar, I am among the first to take seriously the issues and arguments of the new age, to confront the world that is coming before, not the one that has passed from the scene. That is why I hope these few personal remarks, about what it means to be a scholar of Judaism in the free world of universities and what sort of work one does, will show, on a small scale, the dilemma and the opportunity of a whole generation, on a grand scale.

J.N.

Part One
The Paradox of an American Judaism

1
Judaism in Contemporary America

America confronts Judaism with the challenge and opportunity of addressing Jews in a free society. For the long centuries in which Jews lived as a separate and (usually) protected minority, from ancient times to the nineteenth century, Judaism constructed a way of life and expressed a world view for a social group whose persistence seldom was called into question. From their beginnings Christianity and Islam always recognized the legitimacy (if the inferiority, too) of Judaism, which Jews took to be self-evident. To be sure, Jews found their lives and property threatened. But Judaism could explain that fact and so find even reinforcement in it. More important, memories of times of stress flowed together with the experience of a world in which Jews found themselves living mainly among other Jews, by both mutual consent and political constraint. In America by contrast the Jews' life together as a distinct group has come to depend mainly upon inner assent, produced in decisions of individuals to make something of their origin. As time has passed, "being Jewish" has resulted less and less from external compulsion. The reason is that in the condition of the open and free society constructed by Americans, Jews really did not find themselves much different from others. Moreover, the distinguishing traits — whether imposed or voluntary — of a Jewish language, Jewish clothing, Jewish occupations, and Jewish places of residence, which had marked the immediate predecessors of American Jews in Central and Eastern Europe, were absent in America from the very beginning. Consequently, Jews, and therefore Judaism, found themselves in a circumstance hitherto not common in their history.

Freedom's Challenge to Judaism

The condition of freedom overtook the Jews only slowly, and then by generations. The numerous immigrants of the later nineteenth and early twentieth centuries (from 1880 to 1920, more than 3.5 million Jews came to the United States from Russia, Poland, Romania, Hungary, and Austria) spoke Yiddish all their lives. They pursued a limited range of occupations. They lived mainly in crowded Jewish neighborhoods in a few great cities. So the facts of language, occupation, and residence reinforced their separateness. Judaism then explained it. In this period, moreover, other immigrant groups, together with their churches, also found themselves constituting tight enclaves of the old country in the new. How much freedom of choice a Yiddish-speaking Jewish immigrant from Poland actually exercised, or would have wanted to recognize, surely is limited. The children of the immigrants, that is, the second generation in America, by contrast, adopted the American language and American ways of life. But the second generation grew up and lived in a period of severe anti-Semitism at home and in Europe, especially in the 1930s and 1940s. While trying to forget the immigrant heritage, the second generation found the world a school for Jewish consciousness, and that of a distinctively negative sort. Coming to maturity in the depression and in World War II, the second generation did not have to decide whether or not to "be Jewish," nor were they forced to make many decisions about what "being Jewish" meant.

That set of decisions, amounting to the framing of a situation of genuine free choice, awaited the third generation, reaching its maturity after World War II. That generation felt little psychological pressure, compared to what its predecessors had faced, in favor of "being Jewish." Surveys of anti-Semitic feeling turned up progressively diminishing levels of Jew hatred. More important, while the second generation had strong memories of Yiddish-speaking parents and lives of a distinctly Jewish character, the third generation in the main did not. For in line with Hanson's law, the second generation made a vigorous effort to forget what it knew. The third generation had to make a decision to learn what it did not know, indeed, what it had no natural reason, in its upbringing and family heritage, to know. American Judaism as we know it today is the creation of that third generation, the result of its conscientious effort to remember what its parents equally deliberately forgot. The decision was made in a free society and represented free and uncoerced choice. So the third generation forms the first generation of Judaism in a long series of centuries to be able to decide in an open society whether or not to be Jewish. More interesting, it is the first generation to define for itself what "being Jewish" would consist of, and how Judaism, as an inherited and received religious tradition, would be taken over as part of this definition.

The Generations of American Judaism

How so? To understand how the third generation of American Jews defined for itself a distinctive and fresh Judaic system, that is, a world view and way of life serving a distinct social group or class, we must examine a striking contrast. It is between the state of Judaism at the point at which the second generation (1920–1950) had defined matters, and the equivalent condition of Judaism for the third generation (1950–1980) thirty years later, hence between the Judaism of the 1940s and 1950s and the Judaism of the 1970s and 1980s. Beginning, for purposes of comparison and contrast, with the latter, we find a vast network of educational activities in Judaism, both formal and informal. There are, for example, camps devoted to the use of the Hebrew language in both prayer and everyday activities, youth groups, and programs of Judaic interest in Jewish community centers. A system of Judaic schooling based on afternoon and Sunday sessions now competes with the more intensive all-day schooling of Jewish parochial schools, many under Orthodox, some under Conservative auspices. The organized Jewish community in its philanthropic activities invests sizable sums in Judaic activities, youth programs, camps, and formal schooling. The religious observances of classical Judaism in Orthodox, Conservative, Reform, and Reconstructionist modes reach beyond the synagogue into the home, on the one side, and into formal community programs, on the other. Important historical events, such as the destruction of the Jews of Europe ("the Holocaust," in English, *Shoah,* in Hebrew), receive massive community attention and commemoration. Even a program of quasi-religious pilgrimage, in the form of study trips to the Holy Land, the State of Israel, draws large numbers of participants from the community, old and young. Jewish organizations of an other-than-religious orientation (it is difficult to regard them as wholly secular) undertake these travel programs, generally imparting to them a strong religious-educational aspect. These same supposedly secular organizations include in their programs study sessions of a decidedly religious character, in which the Hebrew Scriptures and other Judaic texts or events of sacred history play an important role. Surveys of religious observance confirm a fairly broad level of popular participation in at least some Judaic rites, such as the Passover Seder, though many other rites have become mere curiosities. Finally, alongside the neo-Judaic activism of the third generation comes the foundation, in the American Jewish community, of a quite distinct generation. Now a new first generation takes root, this one made up of survivors of the European catastrophe who came to the United States in the late 1940s and early 1950s, with yet more recent immigrants from the State of Israel and Asian countries, on the one side, and the Soviet Union, on the other. The new first generation, beginning with its own history, has founded a broad range of vigorously Orthodox institutions and created a quite separate life for itself, in which Judaism as a classical religion defines the affairs of culture and society in every detail. The new first generation has had a deep impact on the Orthodoxy of the third generation. It must be said that by the mid-1980s, therefore, a distinctively American expression of Judaism had come to full realization. What this meant is that a set of Judaic systems has come to definition in this country. Those who have defined them clearly have found effective ways of transmitting, to a fourth and a fifth and a sixth generation, a rooted and ongoing Judaism made in America.

Why that fact is noteworthy has now to be spelled out. The first generation (1890–1920), completing its migration and settling down in the 1920s, took for granted that its ways would not continue. How do we know? Because they did not try to preserve Yiddish. The Yiddish language *within* the first generation gave way to English, often in the home, and with it went much else that had seemed definitively Jewish in the Central and East European setting. With the notion that Jews (like other immigrants) must become American, the immigrant generation tended to accept, not always willingly to be sure, what it perceived as the de-Judaization of its children. The parents kept the dietary taboos, the children did not. The parents practiced distinctly Jewish occupations, dominating only a few fields and absent in most others. The children spread out, so far as they could in the prevailing climate of anti-Semitism and exclusion. It follows, therefore, that the founding generation of Judaism in America did not define a system of Judaism, let alone a set of such systems, that it imagined it could transmit to the next generation. It contributed in rich and important ways to what the coming generation would inherit and utilize. But it defined nothing, except by negative example: The second generation (1920–1950) wanted to be American, therefore not Jewish. Judaism as an inherited religious tradition with rich theological perspectives and a demanding, enduring way of life bore little relevance to the American children of those Europeans who had walked on that path to God and lived by that mode of sanctification. And the immigrants took that fact for granted.

The second generation, for its part, accepted more from the founders than it planned. For while explicitly opting for "America" and against "Judaism," that generation implicitly defined life as a set of contrasts between the Jewish datum of life, on the one side, and everything else, on the other. Being Jewish was what defined existence for the second generation. That fact of life was so pervasive as not to demand articulation, let alone specific and concrete expression. The upshot was that the second generation would organize bowling leagues and athletic clubs, rather than prayer circles and study groups. But everyone in the bowling league would be Jewish, and they also would be neighbors and friends. The cultural distinctiveness that had char-

acterized the first generation gave way to a Jewishness by association for the second. The associations,
whether political or recreational or philanthropic, took
for granted that the goal was nonsectarian. Little that
proved definitively Jewish would mark the group's
collective life. But how nonsectarian could an association become when all its members lived in pretty much
the same neighborhood, pursued the same lines of
work, and came from Yiddish-speaking parents? In
fact the community life constructed on the basis of
associations characteristic of the second generation
constituted a deeply Jewish mode of life. It took for
granted exactly what the first generation had handed
on, that is, the basic and definitive character of being
Jewish, whatever that might come to mean for the new
generation. The founding generation could not, and
rarely tried to, articulate what being Jewish meant.
But it imparted the very imprint of being Jewish that
it had hoped to leave behind. The second generation
was American and remained Jewish. More than that
the first generation could not imagine.

The second generation did little to found camps,
youth programs, or schools beyond a perfunctory
effort. The institutions of the second generation recognized no need to make explicit, through either sub-
stantive or symbolic means, their Jewish character.
There were few Jewish parochial schools. Jewish community centers regarded themselves as nonsectarian
community agencies. Jewish philanthropic agencies
maintained a high wall of separation between "church"
and "state." The result was that little public Jewish

money went into Judaic activities of any kind. A great
deal went into fighting anti-Semitism and maintaining
nonsectarian hospitals. Proof of these contrasting
modes of Judaic life comes readily to hand. Nearly all
of the Judaizing programs and activities of the third
generation, now received as the norm and permanent,
date back only to the decades after World War II. Most
of the earliest summer camps of Judaic character orig-
inated in that period, especially camps under religious
auspices (as distinct from Zionist and Hebraist ones).
The several youth movements got under way in the
late 1940s. The Jewish federations and welfare funds
in the 1960s fought the battle for a policy of sectarian
investment in distinctively Jewish programs and activities. They undertook to treat as stylish anything
markedly Judaic only from the 1970s. These and equivalent facts point to the passage from the second to the
third generation as the age of decisive redefinition.

Explaining the Generations of Judaism

The factors that account for the shifts in generations
begin in one simple, negative fact. The second generation did not need schools or youth groups in order to
explain what being Jewish meant. Why not? It could
rely on two more effective educational instruments:
memory and experience. The second generation remembered things that the third generation could
scarcely imagine: genuinely pious parents, for example.
But, as we noted earlier, the second generation also
came to maturity in an age in which America turned

against the newest Americans. Universities open to Jews before World War I imposed rigid quotas against them afterward. More important, entire industries declared themselves off-limits to Jewish employment. The fact that the climate of bigotry and exclusion affected others just as much as Jews, so that among the excluded minorities were a majority of Americans of the age, meant little to the excluded Jews. They might have moved in order to swim among an undifferentiated majority if the waters had been open to them; they were not welcome even on the beaches.

Far more profound than the experience of personal exclusion was the impact of the rise of political, organized anti-Semitism as an instrument of national policy in Germany, Poland, and other European countries, with its extension and counterpart in the Western democracies. What this meant was that the exclusion from a country club or an executive suite took on a still more ominous character, as the world at large took up the war against the Jews. Jewish immigration was barred when people fled for their lives. In such a setting Jews scarcely needed to find reasons to associate with one another; the world forced them together. They did not lack lessons on how and why to be Jewish, or on what being Jewish meant. The world defined and taught those lessons with stern and tragic effect. All of the instrumentalities for explaining and propagating Jewishness, created for the third generation, and, in time, by the third generation, would earlier have proved superfluous.

The contrast, then, between the second and the third

generations sets up the encounter with a hostile and threatening world, on the one side, against the experience of an essentially neutral and benign one, on the other. Yet that contrast proves somewhat misleading. For three other factors contributed to the renaissance of articulated and self-conscious Jewishness, along with a renewed search for Judaism, among third-generation Americans of Jewish descent. The first was the rise of the State of Israel. The second was the discovery, not of the murder of nearly six million Jews in Europe, but of "the Holocaust." The third was the "reethnicization" of American life, that is, the resurgence of ethnic identification among the grandchildren of the immigrant generations, on the one side, and among blacks and other excluded groups that long ago had become American by force, on the other. Just as the Jewish third generation tried to remember what the second generation had wanted to forget, so other groups followed the same pattern elsewhere. Just as black students demanded what they deemed ethnically characteristic food, so Jewish students discovered they wanted kosher food.

All three factors reinforced one another among the Jews. We take as routine the importance of the State of Israel in American Jewish consciousness. But in the 1940s and 1950s, American Jewry had yet to translate its deep sympathy for the Jewish state into political activity, on the one side, and into local cultural activity and sentiment, on the other. So too the memory of the destruction of European Jewry did not right away become known as the Holocaust, as a formative event in contemporary Jewish consciousness. In fact the re-ethnicization of the Jews could not have taken the form that it did — a powerful identification with the State of Israel as the answer to the question of the Holocaust — without a single, catalytic event.

The 1967 War: American Israel and Israeli Messianism

That single, catalytic event was the 1967 war between the State of Israel and its Arab neighbors. When, on June 5, after a long period of threat, the dreaded war of "all against one" began, American Jews feared the worst. Six days later they confronted an unimagined outcome, with the State of Israel standing on the Jordan River, the Nile, and the outskirts of Damascus. The trauma of the weeks preceding the war, when the Arabs promised to drive the Jews into the sea and no other power intervened or promised help, renewed for the third generation the nightmare of the second. Once more the streets and newspapers became the school for being Jewish. What do I mean? In the 1930s and 1940s, the age of Hitler's Germany and the murder of the European Jews in death factories, everyday the newspaper brought lessons of Jewish history. Everybody knew that if he or she were in Europe, death would be the sentence for the crime of Jewish birth. And the world was then indifferent. No avenues of escape were opened to the Jews who wanted to flee, and many roads to life were deliberately blocked by anti-Semitic foreign service officials in the United

States, Canada, and other democracies. So too in 1967
the Arab states threatened to destroy the State of Israel
and murder its citizens. The Israelis turned to the
world. The world again ignored Jewish suffering, and
a new "Holocaust" began. But this time the outcome
was different. The entire history of the century at
hand came under a new light. As we shall see below, a
moment of powerful and salvific weight placed into a
fresh perspective everything that had happened from
the beginning to the present.

The third generation had found its memory and its
hope. It now could confront the murder of the Jews
of Europe, along with its parents' (and, for not a few,
its own) experience of exclusion and bigotry. No longer
was it necessary to avoid painful, intolerable memories.
Now what had happened had to be remembered, because it bore within itself the entire message of the new
day in Judaism. Relating the murder of nearly six million Jews of Europe to the creation of the State of
Israel transformed both events. One became known as
the Holocaust, the purest statement of evil in all of
human history. The other became salvation in the form
of "the first appearance of our redemption" (as the
language of the Jewish prayer for the State of Israel
has it). Accordingly, a moment of stark epiphany cap-
tured the entire experience of the age and imparted
to it the meaning and order that a religious system has
the power to express and make self-evident. The self-
evident system of American Judaism, then, for the
third generation encompassed a salvific myth deeply
and personally relevant to the devotees. That myth

made sense, at a single instant, equally of both the world and the self, of what the newspapers had to say, and of what the individual understood in personal life.

The distinctively American form of Judaism under description here is clearly connected to classical Judaism. But it is not continuous with it. American Judaism draws upon some of the received religious tradition and claims to take up the whole of it. But in its stress upon the realization, in the here and now, of ultimate evil and salvation, and in its mythicization of contemporary history, American Judaism offers a distinctively American, therefore a new and unprecedented, reading of the received tradition. This is by definition. For when Jews have come to speak of fully realized salvation and an end of history, the result has commonly proved to be a new religion, connected to, but not continuous with, the received religion of Judaism. That is very much the case even now.

The ambiguity of American Judaism lies in sorting out what is old from what is new, in discovering, in the continuation of the familiar, what has changed, and in determining, in what appears to be new, what turns out to be entirely familiar and well attested for centuries. In order to accomplish this work of analysis, we proceed to consider each of the primary categories of the received version of Judaism. When we allow the Judaism brought from Europe to tell us how to organize our data, we must speak of the categories from which that system for a social group had constructed its world view and expressed that world view through a distinctive way of life. The simple categories, each beyond reduction to any more general or encompassing one, are these: (1) way of life (including everyday mode of social organization, types of religious leadership) and (2) world view (where we are, what we believe). These then, in detail, allow us to speak of a holy way of life, holy man, holy people, and holy land. Our task is now to describe that distinctive system of Judaism produced in America, in particular by the third generation for the fourth and fifth generations, in terms of the categories just now defined.

Holy Way of Life

In archaic Judaism the holy life — the things one did to conform to the will of God, or, in secular terms, the behavior patterns imposed by the Judaic tradition — was personal and participative. Every man, woman, and child had myriad deeds to do because he or she was a Jew. No one was exempt from following the holy way of living. Everyone expected to share in it equally. One did not speak of how others should keep the Sabbath. One kept the Sabbath, along with everyone else in the community. People individually said their own prayers, advanced their own education in the tradition, did good deeds on their own part. Prayer, study, and the practice of good deeds were personal and universal. To be a Jew meant to do a hundred *mitzvot,* holy actions, every day.

In modern America, to be a Jew primarily means to

join an organization, but not personally to affect its purposes. The individual is lost in the collectivity. Joining means paying dues, providing sufficient funds so that other people may be hired to carry out the purposes of the organization. The "joining" is the opposite of what it means, for it is impersonal and does not bring people together, but verifies their separateness. The relationship of one person to the next is reduced to the payment of money. It is passive, for one does not actually do much, if anything at all. Universally condemned by the preachers, "checkbook Judaism" is everywhere the norm. What has happened is that the primary mode of being Jewish — living the "holy life" — has moved from the narrow circle of home, family, and small group to the great arena of public affairs and large institutions. But this move has consequences. The formation of large organizations, characteristic of modern life, tends to obliterate the effective role of the individual. In the Judaic situation, even the synagogue, with its substantial budget and massive membership, its professional leadership and surrogate religiosity, follows this pattern. If to be a Jew now means to take an active part in the "Jewish community," then the holy life is lived chiefly by paying one's part of the budget of the organizations that call themselves the community. By contrast, Jews in other countries identify being Jewish with either synagogue membership (at home, in Johannesburg or Sydney or London) or becoming an Israeli (by emigrating to the State of Israel or by focusing one's Jewish life mainly

upon Israeli matters), or both. In general, both modes
of being Jewish involve personal participation, not
simply giving money.

People join organizations because they have been
convinced that that is what "Judaism" expects of
them. They think this primarily because of the patterns
established, or already imposed, by others. The result
is the concentration of power in the hands of a few
individuals who actually determine what organizations
do. These few are not democratically elected, but generally emerge from an oligarchy of wealthy and in-
fluential men (only a few women are included). But
even these men do not actually carry out the work of
the community. They raise the funds and allocate
them, but local funds are in fact spent by, and chiefly
upon the salaries of, the professional bureaucrats
trained to do whatever it is that the organizations do.
In general the organizational work of the prominent
few is to keep the organization alive and prosperous.

What has all this to do with "being Jewish"? Should
we not have started with an account of what "the
Jews believe" or what "Judaism teaches"? Indeed we
should, if what Jews believed and what classical Judaism taught decisively shaped the contemporary realities that define what, in everyday life, it means to be
a Jew. Since we ask what it means to be a Jew in America, the first thing we want to know is: What do people
do because they are Jewish? And the answer is: They
join organizations and give money. In this respect,
what makes a person *Jewish* in American society pri-

marily depends on which organization he or she joins and to what worthy cause he or she gives money.

That the "holy way" should have become the "culture of organizations" tells us that modernity has overtaken the Jews. What characterizes group life in modern times is the development of specialists for various tasks, the organization of society for the accomplishment of tasks once performed individually and in an amateur way, the growth of professionalism, the reliance upon large institutions. What modern humanity gains in greater efficiency and higher levels of competence cannot be given up because of nostalgia for a way of life few now living in a traditional society would want to preserve. But as everyone recognizes, the cost of "progress" is impersonality and depersonalization. The real question is not whether to return to a more primitive way of living, but how to regain the humanity, personalism, individual self-respect, and self-reliance necessarily lost from the new way.

Holy Man

The "professional Jews" who run the Jewish institutions and organizations that constitute for the ordinary folk the "holy way" are anonymous, faceless, wholly secular. People relate to them no differently from the way they do to other bureaucrats, in government offices, public schools, department stores. Yet the common people continue to regard one Jewish functionary as quintessentially "Jewish," important, and crucial in the development of values, and this one is the least powerful and least effective figure — the rabbi. For nearly twenty centuries the rabbi was the holy man of Judaic tradition. He became a rabbi through study of the Torah, which comprehended not only the Hebrew Scriptures but also the Oral Torah, believed to have been handed on in Mosaic revelation and eventually recorded in the pages of the Babylonian Talmud and related literature. The rabbi was a holy man consecrated not by prayer, though he prayed, nor by asceticism, though he assumed taxing disciplines, but by study and knowledge of the Torah. That knowledge made him not merely learned or wise but a saint, and endowed him with not only information but also insight into the workings of the universe. Consequently, in former times rabbis were believed to have more than commonplace merits, therefore more than ordinary power over the world, and some of them, especially qualified by learning and piety, were thought to be able to pray more effectively than common people and to accomplish miracles.

Today the rabbi (now both women and men) will be an essentially peripheral figure in organized Jewish life, outside the framework of the synagogue. Dropping the rabbi out of the decision-making circles of the Jewish community merely took account of the rabbi's profoundly different role. Formerly judge, administrator, holy man, scholar, and saint, the rabbi in American Judaism at first served as a rather secular leader of a rather secular community, spokesman for Jews to Gentiles, representative of his synagogue to the larger Jewish group, agent of Zionist propaganda, and certifier of the values of the upper-class Jews who employed him. But as time passed these roles and tasks passed into the hands of others, better equipped for them because of community position, economic power, and public acceptance. By the 1950s a truly professional Jewish civil service was in control in the more enlightened communities. The rabbi was left to preside at circumcisions, weddings, and funerals, to "conduct" religious worship, which, in traditional synnagogues, meant to announce pages and tell people when to stand up and sit down, to counsel the troubled, and to teach the children, in all a slightly anachronistic figure, a medicine man made obsolete by penicillin.

But that is not the whole story. With the decline of the effectiveness of educational enterprises, the rabbi, who normally was perhaps the only Jew in town who could read Hebrew and intelligently comprehend a Jewish book, stood apart for the same reason as in classical times. He was distinguished by his learning. As long as access to Judaic tradition and the ability to comprehend Judaic thinking proved important, the rabbi continued to hold the key to the mind and intellect of Judaism. Still more important, though the rabbi could be made into a pathetic remnant of ancient glories of his office, he remained the rabbi. The title and the role persisted in setting the rabbi apart from others, in making him a kind of holy man. In psychological terms, he continued to function as a surrogate father and God. Secularity did not, could not in the end, deprive him of his role as a religious figure,

even leader. The holy man remained just that, even to
the most secular people.

Today, the rabbi serves primarily his or her congregation. In a sense the rabbi has become a more religious figure than in earlier decades. That means, to be sure, rabbis have less power in Jewish communal affairs. But it is likely that they now enjoy more *influence* than before, and influence in shaping the ideas and purposes of others represents significant power to achieve concrete ends. The rabbi does not stand at the head of organizations, of community bureaus. But the rabbi stands behind those who do, for Jewish leaders nearly universally belong to synagogues and rely upon religious rites at least at the time of life crises — birth, puberty, marriage, death. They are accessible to the rabbi's words.

Above all, community leaders are under the spell of the rabbi as a holy person, in a way in which the passing generation was not. To be sure, lay people are as well educated as the rabbi in many ways. But in respect to the knowledge of Judaism, standards of literacy have so fallen that the rabbi now dominates in precisely the one area appropriate to his calling. So far as people remain Jews, they depend more than ever upon rabbis to explain to them why they should act in a certain way and what this or another act means. It is the rabbi who retains the prestige and the learning to fill that empty commitment of Jews to being Jewish with purpose and meaning.

The real foundations for the rabbinical position are the convictions people retain from archaic times about holy men, set aside for God and sanctified by sacred disciplines. In archaic times the rabbi was a holy man because of his mastery of the Torah. Today the rabbi remains a holy man for that very reason. Thus far we have seen the sociological side of that holiness: The rabbi continues functionally to dominate because of his knowledge of the Torah. With women now included, the rabbi has new opportunities for effective contemporary service.

The advent of women to the Reform rabbinate has already given the Reform sector of the Jewish community access to talent formerly excluded from the pulpit. With the ordination of women in the Conservative rabbinate and the Reconstructionist one as well, the vast majority of American Jews — certainly 80 percent of the whole — now turn to women, as much as to men, as authority figures in Judaism. The renewed energy flowing from the formerly excluded half of the Jewish people already has made its mark. Women in synagogues find themselves more normal, more at home, than they could when only men occupied liturgical and other positions of symbolic importance and real power. Highly talented young women aspire to the rabbinate who formerly would have chosen other callings or professions. In these and other obvious ways, the advent of women to the rabbinate has redefined the profession and renewed its promise.

Holy People

The "holy people" in archaic times certainly knew who they were and confidently defined their relationship with Gentiles. Jews saw themselves as Israel, the people to whom the Torah had been revealed, now living in exile from their homeland. Israel was a nation within other nations. But eventually Israel would return to the Holy Land, with the coming of the Messiah. Gentiles were outsiders, strangers to be respected but feared, honored but avoided except when necessary. Modern times were different. From the nineteenth century onward Western European Jews consciously entered the society of the nations among which they had lived for generations. They became German, French, and British citizens, ceased to form a separate community, and sought normal relationships both with Gentiles and with their culture.

For the immigrants to America the nineteenth-century Western European experience repeated itself. At first the Jews formed separate, Yiddish-speaking enclaves in large cities, but as time passed they and their children moved to less uniformly Jewish neighborhoods, entered less characteristically Jewish occupations, and wholeheartedly adopted the language and culture of the America they had chosen. The assimilation of Jews into American culture continued apace in the second generation, and by the third it was virtually complete. We shall see the evidence when we consider the problem of self-hatred (chapter 7). Then the questions became, and remain, What is a Jew? Who is Israel? What makes a person into a Jew? Are the Jews a religious group? Are they a "people"? A nation? The Jews thus have entered a lingering crisis of group identity; that is, they are not certain who they are or what is being asked of them because of what they claim to be. And individual Jews face a severe dilemma of personal identity as well: Why should I be a Jew? What does it mean, if anything, that I am born of Jewish parents?

One important measure of modernity is the loss of the old certainties about who one is. The question of who is a Jew, always chronic, became critical in the 1940s and 1950s. The sense of a "crisis of identity" is a condition of being a modern person. Formerly, people suppose, men and women were confident of their place in the life of the community and certain of the definition of that community in the history of mankind. To be a Jew not only imposed social and economic roles but also conveyed a considerable supernatural story. Israel was the people of the Lord, bearer of revelation, engaged in a pilgrimage through history, en route to the promised land at the end of time. To be a Jew was to know not only who one was but also what that meant in the economy of universal history. To identify oneself as a Jew was a privilege and a responsibility, but it was not a problem. The world posed problems to the Jew, particularly in the 1930s and 1940s; Judaism and "being Jewish," not separated from one another, solved those problems, explained felt history, interpreted everyday reality in terms of a grand and encompassing vision of human history and destiny. "We are Israel, children of Abraham, Isaac, and Jacob, loyal sons of the Torah of Moses at Sinai, faithfully awaiting the anointed of God." What difference did it make that Gentiles treated Jews contemptuously, despised them, maligned their religion? In the end everyone would know the truth. Before the eyes of all the living, God would redeem Israel and vindicate the patience and loyal faithfulness shown in its disagreeable experience in history, among men.

What strikingly characterizes the imagination of the classical Jew, practitioner of Judaism, is the centrality of Israel, the Jewish people, in human history, the certainty that being a Jew is the most important thing about oneself, and that Jewishness, meaning Judaism, was the dominant aspect of one's consciousness. The "holy people" today have disintegrated in the classical formulation. How so? First, Jews are no longer certain just what makes them into a people. Second, they see themselves as anything but holy, they interpret in a negative way the things that make them Jewish and different from others, and above all, they introduce into their assessment of themselves the opinions of the Gentiles. So the advent of modernity seems to have changed everything. A group once sure of itself and convinced of its value under the aspect of eternity now is unsure of who it is and persuaded that the hostile judgments of outsiders must be true. The "children of Abraham, Isaac, and Jacob" have lost touch with the fathers. The people of the Lord seem to have forgotten why as a group they have come into being. Everyday reality contains for ordinary Jews no hint of a great conception of human history. It has become a long succession of meaningless but uncongenial encounters.

Sinai is a mountain. Tourists make the trip to climb it. The "Torah of Moses" is a scroll removed from its holy ark on the Sabbath, normally in the absence of the "loyal sons," who rarely see it, less often hear it, and cannot understand its language. The Messiah at the end of time is too far away to be discerned; in any event, no one is looking in that direction.

It is easy enough to draw invidious contrasts between the virtues of the archaic world and the shortcomings of modernity. But since the old certainties and securities are mostly gone, one might observe that not only necessity but choice moved Jews away from them. When Jews in Eastern Europe began to feel the birth pangs of modernity, especially when the emigrants went to America and plunged into the modern condition, they scarcely looked backward. Whatever virtues they knew in the old way of being did not restrain them. Something in the traditional life seemed to them to have failed, for in their thirst for whatever was new and contemporary they demonstrated that the old had not fulfilled their aspirations.

Orthodoxy

It did not have to be so, and for some it was not. Let me qualify the description I have just given, which leads to the impression that nearly all American Jews had given up on Judaism in its classical and ongoing form, whether mediated through Orthodox or Conservative or Reform synagogues and temples. There

certainly was an Orthodox minority within American
Jewry and not all immigrants tried to raise their children only in English, to speak of both religious and cultural indicators. Orthodoxy characterized nearly all those immigrants who were religious, and Conservative Judaism, a modified form of Orthodoxy, certainly predominated for the second and third generations. Both the emigrants of the 1890s and those who came after World War II included considerable numbers of Jews who remained loyal to the tradition in a wholly traditional way. The appeal of modernity was lost on them. Still others entered the modern situation and quickly turned their backs on it. They returned to classical Judaism. The return to religion in the decades after World War II saw considerable strengthening of Orthodox commitment and conviction in American Judaism, and renascent Orthodoxy did not take the modern form of surrogate religiosity, large synagogues, and impersonal professionalism, but the entirely traditional forms of personal commitment and maximum individual participation. Whether traditional Orthodox Judaism in America is traditional and Orthodox in the same ways as in Eastern European Judaism hardly matters. The fact is that the classical Judaic perspective remains a completely acceptable choice for substantial numbers of American Jews. Those Jews who fully live the traditional life and adhere to the traditional way of faith seem to me to have made a negative judgment on modernity and its values. It becomes all the more striking that larger numbers — the vast ma-

30   jority of American Jewry — came to an affirmative opinion.

But in affirming the modern and accepting its dilemmas, American Jews of the third generation (1950–1980) continued in important modes to interpret themselves in the archaic ways. Most important, Jews continued to see themselves as Jews, to regard that fact as central to their very being, and to persist in that choice. That fact cannot be taken for granted. The Jews are not simply an ethnic group characterized by primarily external, wholly unarticulated and unselfconscious qualities. They are Jewish not merely because they happen to have inherited quaint customs, unimportant remains of an old heritage rapidly falling away. On the contrary they hold strong convictions about how they will continue to be Jews. Most of them hope their children will marry within the Jewish community. Most of them join synagogues and do so because they want their children to grow up as Jews. Above all, most of them find great significance in their being Jewish.

The American Jews of the third generation continue to see everyday life in terms different from their gentile neighbors, beginning with the fact, immensely important to them if not to their neighbors, that they are Jewish. The words they use to explain that fact, the symbols by which they express it, are quite different from those of archaic or classical Judaism. They speak of Jewishness, not of the Torah. They are obsessed with a crisis of identity, rather than with the

tasks and responsibilities of "Israel." They are deeply
concerned with the opinion of Gentiles.

Jewish But Not Too Jewish

In all, American Jews of the third generation are eager
to be Jewish — but not too much so, not so much that
they cannot also take their place within the undifferentiated humanity of which they fantasize. They confront
a crisis not merely of identity but of commitment, for
they do not choose to resolve the dilemma of separateness within an open society. In preferring separateness,
they seem entirely within the archaic realm; in dreaming of an open society, they evidently aspire to a true
accomplishment of the early promise of modernity.
But if that truly open society should come to realization, one wonders whether the Jews would want wholly
to enter it. For standing at the threshold of more than
two hundred years of assimilation into modern culture, of facing a lingering crisis of identity, who would
have predicted what has happened? The Jew continues
to take with utmost seriousness the fact of his or her
being Jewish; indeed he or she continues to speak precisely as did those in the classical tradition of Israel.

Holy Land

Archaic religions usually focus upon a holy place,
where God and humanity come together, the focus
for the sacred upon earth. In classical Judaism, Palestine ("the Land of Israel") was not merely the place

where Jews lived, but the Holy Land. It could never legitimately be governed by pagans — thus, the continuing efforts of Jews to drive pagan rulers out of the land. There the Temple was built, the nexus of the God-man relationship in olden times. The mountains of the land were the highest on the earth. The land was the center of the world, of the universe. Jerusalem was most beautiful, most holy.

No element of the classical myth at the turn of the twentieth century could have seemed more remote from the likely preferences of American Judaism when it grew to maturity. When the emigrants left Russia, they could have gone southward, to Palestine, and a few of them did. But most went west, and of these, the largest number went to the United States. Since even then Zionism was an important option in Eastern European Judaism, one can hardly regard the emigrants as Zionists. A few who were Zionists stayed in America only a while, then left for Palestine. The vast majority of emigrants went to America and settled down.

Now, eighty or ninety years later, the vast majority of third and fourth generation American Jews support the State of Israel, and whether they are called Zionists hardly matters. The sole commitment shared by nearly all, uniquely capable of producing common action, is to the continuation of the State of Israel. Zionism accounts for the major portion of the welfare funds. To American Jews, the phrase "never again" — referring to the slaughter of nearly six million European Jews — means that the State of Israel must not be permitted to perish. But there is a second, less often articulated fact about American Jewry. Alongside the nearly universal concern for the State of Israel is — by definition — the quite unanimous Jewish commitment to America, to remain Americans. Emigration from the United States to the State of Israel since 1948 has been negligible. Indeed, until the present time five times more Israelis have settled in America than American Jews in Israel.

Clearly, Zionism, with its focus upon the State of Israel, solves problems for American Jews. How does it do so, and why, then, do American Jews in the vast majority find Zionism so critical to their sense of themselves as a "holy people"?

Zionism provides a reconstruction of Jewish identity, for it reaffirms the nationhood of Israel in the face of the disintegration of the religious bases of a Jewish "peoplehood." If in times past the Jews saw themselves as a people because they were the children of the promise, the children of Abraham, Isaac, and Jacob, called together at Sinai, instructed by God through prophets, led by rabbis guided by the "whole Torah" — written and oral — of Sinai, then with the end of a singularly religious self-consciousness, the people lost their understanding of themselves as a people. The fact is that the people remained a community of fate, but until the flourishing of Zionism, the facts of their continued existence were deprived of a heuristic foundation. Jews continued as a group, but could not persuasively say why, or what this meant. Zionism provided the explanation: The Jews indeed remain a people, but the basis for their self-perception as a people lies in the unity of their concern for Zion, their devotion to rebuilding the land and establishing Jewish sovereignty in it. The realities of continuing emotional and social commitment to separateness as Jews thus made sense. Mere secular difference, once seen to be destiny — "who has not made us like the nations" — once again stood forth as destiny.

The Ambiguity of Zionism

Herein lies the ambiguity of Zionism. It was supposedly a secular movement, yet in reinterpreting the classical mythic structures of Judaism, it compromised its secularity and exposed its fundamental unity with like attributes that do not necessarily represent "peoples" or "nations," and if the common attributes, in the Jewish case, are neither intrinsically Jewish (whatever that might mean) nor widely present to begin with, then the primary conviction of Zionism constitutes an extraordinary reaffirmation of the primary element in the classical mythic structure: salvation. What has happened in Zionism is that the old has been in one instant destroyed and resurrected. The "holy people" are no more, the nation-people take their place. How much has changed in the religious tradition when the allegedly secular successor-continuer has preserved not only the essential perspective of the tradition, but done so pretty much in the tradition's own symbols and language?

Nor should it be supposed that the Zionist solution

to the Jews' crisis of identity is a merely theological or ideological one. We cannot ignore the practical result of Zionist success in conquering the Jewish community. For the middle and older generations, as everyone knows, the Zionist enterprise provided the primary vehicle for Jewish identity. The Reform solution to the identity problem — we are Americans by nationality, Jews by religion — was hardly congruent with the profound Jewish passion of the immigrant generations and their children. The former generations were *not* merely Jewish by religion. Religion was the least important aspect of their Jewishness. They deeply felt themselves Jewish in their bone and marrow and did not feel sufficiently marginal as Jews to *need* to affirm their Americanness and Judaism at all. Rather the first and second generations (1890-1950) participated in a reality; they were in a situation so real and intimate as to make unnecessary such an uncomfortable, defensive affirmation. They did not doubt they were Americans. They did not need to explain what being Jewish had to do with it. Zionism for the second generation was congruent with these realities, and because of that, being Jewish and being Zionist were inextricably joined together.

But Zionism also constitutes a problem for Judaism. The mythic insufficiency of Zionism renders its success a dilemma for contemporary American Jews, and for Israeli ones as well. Let us begin with the obvious. How can American Jews focus their spiritual lives *solely* on a land in which they do not live? It is one thing for that land to be in heaven, at the end of time.

It is quite another to dream of a faraway place where everything is good — *but* where one may go if he wants. The realized *eschaton* is insufficient for a rich and interesting fantasy life, and, moreover, in this-worldly terms it is hypocritical. It means American Jews live off the capital of Israeli culture. The "en-landisement" of American Judaism — making Jewish life focus on one place, so the focusing of its imagina-tive, inner life upon the land and State of Israel — therefore imposes an *ersatz* spiritual dimension: "We live here *as if* we lived there — but do not choose to migrate."

Furthermore, it diverts American Judaism from the concrete mythic issues it has yet to solve: Why should anyone be a *Jew* anywhere, in the United States or in Israel? That question is not answered by the recom-mendation to participate in the spiritual adventures of people in a quite different situation. Since the pri-mary *mitzvot* or commandments of American Juda-ism concern supplying funds, encouragement, and support for Israel, one wonders whether one must be a Jew at all in order to believe in and practice that form of Judaism. What is "being Jewish" now supposed to mean?

Jewishness without Judaism?

The underlying problem, which faces both Israeli and American Jews, is understanding what the ambiguous adjective *Jewish* is supposed to mean when the noun *Judaism* has been abandoned. To be sure, for some

Israelis and American Jews, to be a Jew is to be a citizen of the State of Israel — but that definition hardly serves when Israeli Moslems and Christians are taken into account. If one ignores the exceptions, the rule is still wanting. If to be a Jew is to be — or to dream of being — an Israeli, then the Israeli who chooses to settle in a foreign country ceases to be a Jew when he gives up Israeli citizenship for some other. If all Jews are on the road to Zion, then those who either do not get there or, once there, choose another way are to be abandoned. That makes Jewishness depend upon quite worldly issues: This one cannot make his living in Tel Aviv, that one does not like the climate of Afula, the other is frustrated by the bureaucracy of Jerusalem. Are they then supposed to give up their share in the "God of Israel"?

American Jews half a century ago would not have claimed the term *religious* as an appropriate adjective for their community. Today they insist upon it. The moralists' criticism of religion will always render ever more remote what is meant by "true religion," so we need not be detained by carping questions. But can there be religion with so minimal a quotient or supernatural experience, theological conviction, and evocative ritual, including prayer, as is revealed in American Judaism? If one draws the dividing line between belief in a supernatural God and atheism, then much of American Jewry, also much of American Judaism, may stand on the far side of that line. If the dividing line is, in the words of Kristor Stendahl, "between the closed mind and spiritual sensibility and imagination," then American Jews and American Judaism may stand within the frontier of the religious, the sacred.

Let us begin with the substitution of organizations and group activity for a holy way of life lived by each individual. What the Jews have done in their revision of the holy way is to conform to, in their own way to embody, the American talent at actually accomplishing things. Americans organize. They do so, not to keep themselves busy, but to accomplish efficiently and with an economy of effort a great many commendable goals. They hire "professionals" to do well what most individuals cannot do at all: heal the sick, care for the needy, tend the distressed at home and far away. In modern society people do not keep guns in their homes for self-protection. They have police. Nations do not rely upon the uncertain response of well-meaning volunteers. They form armies. The goals American Jews seek to accomplish through their vast organizational life derive from their tradition. They want to educate the young and old, to contribute to the building of the ancient land, to see to it that prayers are said and holidays observed. Now hiring a religious virtuoso may seem less commendable than saying one's own prayers, but it is merely an extension of the specialization people take for granted elsewhere.

Archaic and Modern

In archaic times people believed that salvation depended upon keeping to the holy way, so each person kept to it, made himself sufficiently expert to know

how to carry out the law. In other religious communities today, that same viewpoint persists. Catholics
and Protestants take for granted that they should go
to church to pray. Jews regard communal prayer as
less important, though Judaism has not changed its
position on that matter. They tend to observe the religious way of life in diminishing measure as the generations of American Jews pass on, from third to fourth
to fifth. Today few believe that supernatural salvation
inheres in prayers, dietary taboos, and Sabbath observance. It is therefore curious that the Jews still want
to preserve the old salvific forms and symbols, as they
certainly do. Few pray. Still fewer believe in prayer.
It is astonishing that the synagogues persist in focusing
their collective life upon liturgical functions. Perhaps
the best analogy is to a museum, in which old art is
preserved and displayed, though people do not paint
that way anymore, may not even comprehend what
the painter did, the technical obstacles he overcame.
The synagogue is a living museum and preserves the
liturgical and ritual life of the old tradition. Why should
Jews choose this way, when earlier in their American
experience they seemed to move in a different direction? Is it nostalgia for a remembered, but unavailable
experience of the sacred? Is the religious self-definition
they have adopted merely an accommodation to American expectations? Or do they hope the archaic and
the supernatural may continue to speak to them?

The figure of the rabbi calls forth the same wonder-
ment. Why call oneself rabbi at all if one (man or
woman) is not a saint, a scholar, a judge? Given the

ultimate mark of secularization — the complaint that rabbis no longer reach high places in the Jewish community — should we not ask, "What is still sacred in the rabbi and his or her learning, calling, leadership?" The answer would be, nothing whatsoever, were it not for people's relationships to the rabbi, their fantastic expectations of him or her. The rabbi may be unsure of his or her role, at once self-isolated and complaining about his or her loneliness — yet whatever he is, he is the rabbi. He knows it. The people know it. They look to him as a kind of holy man. No nostalgia here: The rabbi is a completely American adaptation of the ancient rabbinical role. But American society never imposed the peculiar, mainly secular definition of "Jewish clergyman" upon the modern rabbi. For two hundred years American Jewry had no rabbis at all. Leadership lay with uneducated men, businessmen mainly. And the rabbis they now have are not merely Judaic versions of Protestant ministers or Roman Catholic priests, but uniquely Judaic as well as exceptionally American. The remembrance of rabbis of past times — of the saints, scholars, and holy men of Europe — hardly persists into the fourth generation and beyond. The rabbi, profane and secular, is the holy man or woman they shall ever know. So onto him or her they fix their natural, human fantasies about men and women set apart by and for God.

The holy people, Israel, of times past has become "the American Jewish community," uncertain what is Jewish about itself, still more unsure of what the word

Jewish ought to mean at all. Surely the lingering crisis of self-definition marks the Jew as utterly modern and secular, but we must add to that the second component of the holy people's self-understanding: concern for what the Gentiles think of Jews, readiness to admit that negative opinion into the Jewish assessment of the Jews. This submission to universal opinions and values hardly characterizes a holy people. Frail and uncomfortable, hating those "Jewish traits" in oneself that set Jews apart from everyone else, and wanting to be Jewish but not too much, not so much that they cannot also be undifferentiated Americans — does this describe the holy people who traversed thirty-five centuries of human history, proud, tenacious, alone? Can they claim their collectivity to be holy, separate, and apart? Surely in the passage from the sacred to the secular, the holy people have disintegrated, become a random group of discrete, scarcely similar individuals. Yet while that may seem to be so, the one point Jews affirm is that they shall be Jews. This they have in common.

The very vigor of their activity together and the commonalities of a quite discrete folk suggest that the group, once a people, is still a people. The secular separateness of the Jews, their inner awareness of being a group, their outward view of themselves as in some ways apart from others — that separateness is probably all modern man can hope for socially to approximate "the holy." The archaic "holy people" have passed from the scene. In their place stands something different in all respects but the most important: the manifest and correct claim to continue as Jews, a different, separate group, *and* the claim that that difference is destiny.

The relationship between secular Zionism and sacred messianism, modern nation building and the myth of the return to Zion at the end of time, is complex. It seems clear that the pattern recurs, perhaps most vividly, in the modern and secular modulation of the myth of the Holy Land.

The Torah in American Israel

Let us end with attention to doctrine, the Torah in the mythic language of Judaism. The grandchildren of Jews who would not have understood what theologians do are today those who not only write theology but correctly claim it to be Judaic. The third generation produced religious intellectuals. This is the decisive evidence that something new has been created out of something old. Contemporary American Judaism, for all its distance from the classical forms of the past, its unbelief and secularity, constitutes a fundamentally new and autonomous development, not merely the last stages in the demise of something decadent. American Judaism calls forth, in the task of formulating a systematic account of its faith, the talents of philosophical sophistication and religious conviction, able to speak in the name, even in the words, of the classical tradition, but in a language alien to that tradition. To be sure, the Jews' response to Judaic theology thus far is routine and inconsequential. The best books reach a tiny audience, the worst only a slightly larger one. The finest theological journals are read chiefly by those who write for them, or aspire to. So the theological movement must stand by itself, as evidence of the modernity and secularity of the theologicans, on the one side, but of their participation in the traditional sacred values and in the archaic texts, on the other.

American Judaism constitutes something more than the lingering end of old ways and myths. It is the effort of modern men and women to make use of archaic ways and myths in the formation of a religious way of living appropriate to an unreligious time and community. Spiritual sensibility and, even more, the remnants of the archaic imagination are the sources for the unarticulated, but evident decision of American Jews to reconstruct out of the remnants of an evocative, but incongruous heritage the materials of a humanly viable, meaningful community of life. To have attempted the reconstitution of traditional villages in the metropolis and of archaic ways of seeing the world in the center of modernity would have been to deny the human value and pertinence of the tradition itself. But few wanted even to try. In the end the effort would have had no meaning. The Jews had the courage to insist that their life together must have more than ordinary meaning. In American Judaism they embarked upon the uncertain quest to find, if necessary to invent, to build that meaning. Despite their failures,

44   the gross, grotesque form they have imposed upon the old tradition, that uncommon, courageous effort seems to me to testify to whatever is good and enduring in modernity. But whether good or not, abiding or ephemeral, all that modern men and women have, and all that they shall ever have, is the mature hope to persist in that quest.

Part Two
Israel and the State of Israel

2

Who Is Israel?

The election of Menahem Begin in 1977 brought to the fore the deeply religious, even messianic, attitude toward the State of Israel held by Jews both in the state and abroad. That attitude now flourishes. The notion that annexation is liberation, the claim that God gave us the land and therefore it is ours, transfers clearly theological issues to the political arena. Is Zionism Judaism? If not, what *is* the relationship between Judaism and Zionism?

To understand the attitudes of American Jews toward the State of Israel you need a taste for ambiguity and irony. The ambiguity is in the meaning of the words *state* and *Israel;* the irony, in the passionate engagement with the destiny of the Holy Land on the part of people who are passionately American, deeply secular in the commonplace sense of the word, and uncommonly perplexed by the meaning of their own identity as Jews.

On the one side, the nearly unanimous concern for the welfare of the State of Israel — the Jewish state — on the part of American Jewry is interpreted as support of the old country by an ethnic group, with its parallels extending from Greek-American concern for Cyprus to the Anglo-American concern for Britain that led to our involvement in the Great War. Accordingly, Jews are an ethnic group and express a perfectly natural, and American, ethnic attitude.

On the other side, Jews themselves insist that they form a religious group, and that Zionism constitutes an integral expression of Judaism. It follows that Jews are a churchly community and that the State of Israel represents, not their "old country" (which it isn't), but their Vatican. This latter approach, of course, poses its own complications. Who ever heard of a Baptist national homeland? And when did Roman Catholics last demonstrate on behalf of paper governance of a slice of the Tiber's shore?

Yet if the perceived connection — indeed, the powerful sense of shared destiny — between the Jews of the American diaspora and the State of Israel is not to be interpreted as religious, it surely is more than ethnic. The language associated with the State of Israel is the language of redemption. The hopes evoked are expressed in the imagery of classical Judaic messianism. The ancient prayers for the restoration of Zion — meant, in olden times, to express the messianic hope for the end of days — today are indistinguishable from prayers for the welfare of the State of Israel, containing phrases such as "the beginning of the sprouting forth of redemption."

But that merely lead to the further, perplexing question of whether Zionism is a Jewish mode of secular nationalism or a secular mode of Jewish messianism. The millennial and chiliastic emotions; the invocation of prophetic images of the end of days; the association, with the State of Israel, of the destiny of "the kingdom of priests and the holy people" of theological discourse; and the unnuanced allegation that "Zionism is Judaism" — these argue for the latter view, that Zionism is a secular mode of Jewish messianism.

Yet what can be *religious* about a state? From the Protestant perspective, Judaism is engaged in a kind of neo-Erastianism; from the Roman Catholic perspective, the ancient Israel after the flesh has confused the city of God with the city of man. The principal Western modes of Christianity scarcely understand this heightened sense of spirituality lavished by their Jewish friends and neighbors upon what to them is merely another secular state.

Unraveling the skein of ambiguity begins in the recognition that one person's act of religion is another person's secularism. What is an act of religious piety to a Roman Catholic is a work of idolatry to a Protestant of a certain sort. What Christians long ago declared a matter of private conscience — the eating of pork, for example — is of importance in Judaism and Islam. For *religion* is a word that refers to different things in different "religions." The West fought the Hundred Years' War before it found peace in the secularization of the state. It took another two hundred years to establish the proposition that nationality and religion are distinguished from one another.

For the religions of the Middle East (Islam, Judaism, and the Eastern forms of Christianity), by contrast, religion defines nationality, and nationality, religion.

Consider the State of Israel, with its law that matters of personal status — marriage, divorce, and the like — are settled by the authorities of church, mosque, or synagogue. And going no further from Israel than Lebanon, the "Christian" armies there seem incongruous to Western Protestants and Catholics, and the use of the cross as a military emblem an anachronism (if not blasphemy). And indeed it is, except in the lands untouched by the Reformation and the Catholic Renaissance of the early centuries of our modernity.

Judaism, for its part, seriously entered the West only when large numbers of Jews migrated from the lands of Eastern Europe. In the vast Jewries of Poland, the Ukraine, Lithuania, White Russia, Hungary, and the southern Slavic territories, to be a Jew was to dress in a certain way, eat in a certain way, and pray in a certain way, and so it was also for members of the diverse forms of Christian nationality. The Jews had their own language and vastly articulated culture, forming a distinctive nationality and religion as well. There was no separating the two. They were a nation of one religion, and theirs was a religion of one nation.

Entering the West — and this means, principally, entering America and Canada three generations ago — the Jews in the thirty years of a generation (e.g., 1890–1920) had to accommodate themselves to four hundred years of Western cultural history.

To begin with, as I said in chapter 1, the immigrants hardly tried. Their natural inclination was to continue life as if they had not been uprooted. Overcoming the deep sense both of being aliens and of alienation, they reconstructed as best they could the Yiddish civilization of the East on the sidewalks of New York. It was left to their children to become the real Americans. And they did — with a vengeance.

The second generation did not merely give up the heritage of the first — a thousand-year-old heritage of language, culture, and deeply spiritual values. It deliberately obliterated that ancient civilization through a conscious act of forgetting. The children not only spoke American, they became American by deliberately forgetting that they were also something else and by feigning ignorance of the fact that no one else believed they weren't. For the other Americans didn't perceive the Jewish Americans as very American. The decades of the second generation, from about 1920 to about 1945, witnessed the exclusion of the Jews from the mainstream of American life and the unembarrassed expression of anti-Semitism in institutions of cultural and economic life.

The third generation therefore put on a new cloak: to be American in all ways but religion. To be Jewish now meant to be a kind of American, differentiated solely by matters of religious faith. And Judaism was understood to be a kind of religion not different in its deep structures and definitive traits from other American religions. Will Herberg spelled all this out in his classic work *Protestant-Catholic-Jew* (1957), showing that the three "religions of democracy" had been forced into a common American mold. That other side of "being Jewish" — the side excluded from the category of religion by the prevailing understanding of what a religion could and could not contain — was kept hidden.

The consensus of the third generation, then, may be simply stated once more: "To be Jewish, but not too much so" — not so much that one could not also find a place in the undifferentiated mass of Americans. It was this consensus that was to fall to pieces in the late 1960s. And it was at that point, principally because of the traumas of 1967 and 1973, that Zionism became a definitive component of the American Jewish world view.

For the children of the third generation took seriously what their parents had set forth rather casually. Inevitably, therefore, the fragile consensus had to break into its conflicting components. For some, not being too Jewish meant not being Jewish at all. The flow out of the Jewish community and into movements of political or religious redemption was torrential. For others, if one was to be Jewish at all, then that meant more than the moderation of learning, the suppression of passion, the benign formality of joining a synagogue but not taking too active a part in its religious activities.

The wheel had come full circle. The religious tradition of Judaism, with its insistence upon the santification of the profane and the requirement of expressing God's will in each and every aspect of everyday life, overspread the limits of permitted religiosity.

The religious way of life defined by Judaism cannot be confined to the walls of the synagogue, on the one side, or to the limits of merely ethical behavior with one's fellow human beings, on the other. Praying and ethics are part of Judaism, but not the whole. Learning in the Torah — the sanctification of the intellect in the service of God's word — has some counterpart in Christianity, but outweighs all else in Judaism. The people of Israel, God's people, are simply not a church, and the meaning of being "Israel" is not to be compared, in its intellectual problematic, to ecclesiology. And, it must be said, the place of the Messiah in the redemption of Israel and the study of Christology have nothing to do with each other.

Christians nonetheless may understand if they try to imagine how things would appear under the following aspect: Israel (meaning, the Jewish people) is God's servant. The suffering of Israel bears meaning for the nations. The redemption of humanity depends upon Israel, whose suffering now will in time gain atonement for the sins of the world, and by whose redemption humanity will be redeemed. Reread Isaiah, chapters 53 and 54, and understand that they refer to the Jewish people. At that point — if you can do it — you will enter into the imaginative context of Israel, the Jewish people.

Now back to the present. For a moment I cease to describe, and will tell you my own sense of these matters. When I read those verses, I think only of the Israel after the flesh of which I am part: "He was despised and rejected by men, a man of sorrows and acquainted with grief, and as one from whom men hide their faces; he was despised, and we esteemed him not." Keep in mind the meaning of the extermination of millions of European Jews: "Like a lamb that is led to the slaughter, and like a sheep that before its shearers is dumb, so he opened not his mouth. By oppression and judgment he was taken away; and as for his generation, who considered that he was cut off out of the land of the living, stricken for the transgression of my people?" Kierkegaard struggled with Abraham's willingness to sacrifice his son, Isaac. But in our day Jews had to choose which of their children would live and which would die, and they were not one man but thousands and hundreds of thousands. Our people by oppression and judgment were taken away.

And as for their friends and neighbors, who considered that trainloads of human cargoes crossed Europe to extinction in the East? And who was stricken when a million children, two or three or four years of age, were taken from their parents, and were shoveled directly into the crematoriums, without even prior asphyxiation? The silence of the good Europeans echoes in the silence of America and Britain. We read those words of Isaiah, understood by two millenniums of Christians to refer to Jesus Christ, and we know of whom Isaiah spoke and what he prophesied, and not for one time and one generation only.

For us, therefore, the State of Israel is called by its rightful name, *Israel*. While Jews do not confuse the decisions of the Israeli parliament with the will of God, nearly all understand the state to be something like that "diminished sanctity" of which Ezekiel spoke in the aftermath of the destruction of the First Temple in 586 B.C. And all know that had there been no Holocaust, there also would be no state. None perceives the state as merely of this world, convenient for relocating the remnants of European Jewry and the Jewish refugees from Arab states.

Yet, you rightly object, are Jews not secular? Where are the stigmas of religiosity, to make credible your claim of religious significance for the State of Israel? If you have no religious convictions about other matters, then how are we to grasp what can be religious for you in this one thing? The question is fair; the answer is not easy. For the bulk of Western Jewry — exclusive of Orthodoxy and limited segments of non-Orthodox Judaism — will not concur that to be Jewish is to be a Judaist (that is, a practitioner of Judaism). Jews outside the United States and Canada, and many here as well, do not acknowledge an inexorable tie between being Jewish and confessing Judaism.

At this point one's conception of secularity enters the picture. If you hold that secularity requires a wholly this-worldly and factual interpretation of life, then there is nothing secular about the intense engagement with "being Jewish" — namely, with who is Israel — exhibited by the vast majority of secular Jews. If thirst for salvation and quest for redemption are marks of a truly religious spirit, then what is *not* religious about the messianic hopes and heightened sense of participating in foreordained events characteristic of secular Jews?

If to give for humanitarian purposes is secular (as well as religious), but to sacrifice and focus one's whole being upon the object of sacrifice is a salvific mode of life, then the curiously practical and concrete ways in which Jews center their collective life upon support for the State of Israel surely bear salvific meaning. For the righteousness (bordering, alas, upon self-righteousness) associated with the secular act of supporting the United Jewish Appeal (UJA) or even bonds of the State of Israel is not a secular fact. To those who do these deeds because of "being Jewish," there is nothing secular about them. If you recall that Judaism for its part expresses its beliefs in concrete, practical deeds in the secular world, you will have to concede that, from the viewpoint of Judaism, those who see the UJA as a kind of shrine are not entirely incomprehensible.

And that brings us back to where we started, the problem of understanding the feelings and attitudes of American Jews toward the State of Israel. The ambiguities remain, but we understand how they are generated. The irony of religious passion's being lavished by mainly secular people upon a state, which, like all other states, is a contingent and this-worldly fact, now may be richly enjoyed. Indeed, once you achieve an understanding of this rather curious phenomenon of the larger American culture, you are apt to see ironies and ambiguities where formerly you saw only what is obvious and given, even in the self-evident truths of your own situation.

American Jews in
the State of Israel

What do American Jews have to offer the State of
Israel?

Clearly we must distinguish three groups: American
Jews who settle in the State of Israel, poor and middle-
income American Jews who do not, and rich Jews who
do not.

The last named require no discussion. They have
money. The Israelis know very well how to get it. We
have no advice for them.

The first two groups have something rarer than
money to contribute. They possess both a perception
of the world and of society different from, and lam-
entably absent in, the world outlook of the Israelis,
and the capacity to apply that perception and its formative influences in mediating between the larger
world and the State of Israel.

The special perception of the American Jew is shaped
in an open and democratic society. This perception
understands human relationships accordingly, estab-
lishes expectations of bureaucracy and government as
means of public service, imposes a sense of public responsibility and concern for the common interest. For
let us face facts: A primary difficulty confronting

Americans in the State of Israel is the alien character of its human relations — the truculence of the bureaucracy, the authoritarian aspect of the school system, the government, the universities and other public institutions, and the patent self-interest of unions, political parties, and other small but powerful organized groups in Israeli society.

Israeli perceptions of human relationships in general and of democracy in particular were shaped not in America but in Eastern Europe. It should not be surprising, therefore, that the leaders of an emerging Israeli culture carried with them no clear notion of how democracy works in everyday life. In this connection, the description of Israel's "power elite" in *Transaction* by Rafael Rosenzweig and Georges Tamarin is particularly instructive.

> . . . their ideas (those of second and third *Aliyah*) about human rights and their notions of democracy were somewhat fuzzy. Belonging to a suppressed minority and subscribing to an outlawed political ideology do not provide a good foundation for a deep regard for the next fellow's rights. In addition, the home society of the second and third waves was almost completely lacking in the democratic experience of Western Jewry. They had never seen how a democracy actually works and, though they voiced lofty sentiments about a new society that would be diametrically opposed to the autocratic regimes of their home countries, they in fact developed an autocratic system of their own, based not on wealth but on righteousness.

The point is that Israeli leadership, modeled on the patterns of the second and third *Aliyah* (immigration to the holy land), considers "democracy" to consist simply of proportional representation in the Knesset. But it does not have the foggiest notion that democracy affects the conduct of government, the training of bureaucrats, the planning of educational structures and other mainstays of society. If bureaucrats are rigid and unfeeling, it is because they think they are supposed to be, not because they are less noble in heart than civil servants in other countries. If the educational system operates on the principle that the student is to be kept passive and to be stuffed with facts, that is because it has always been done that way. If the university students are asked to copy down what they hear in lectures and repeat it in writing on examinations, that is because some professors are remembering and repeating what their professors did in Germany, and others, with East European roots, are teaching as did their *melamdim* in *heder*.

What do American immigrants have to contribute? Not a power bloc or pressure group for the revision of institutions and established practices, but rather a new way of doing things within the existing institutions. In this connection I recall a story told to me by Professor Moshe Davis, who left the Jewish Theological Seminary of America to found the Institute of Contemporary Jewry at Hebrew University.

One day early in his Jerusalem sojourn, a student came into his office while he has talking on the phone. He interrupted the call to invite the student to sit down and to say he would be with her in a few minutes. The young woman remained standing, in obvious astonishment. At the end of the call, Davis asked her, "What did I do?" She said, "A professor never asked me to sit down before." The most routine, commonplace courtesy, ingrained by our American teachers, seemed utterly alien in Israel. Multiply this sort of experience many times and you may create a revolution of rising expectations, so to speak — not of wealth or power but of decency and ordinary courtesy.

This is not for one moment to suggest that we are all of one sort, the Israelis of the other. Rather it is to submit that American Jews, along with others from democratic societies of the West, may by their presence and conduct present alternatives to the established way of doing things.

Another thing we have to offer is our uncertainties. Our society has gone through a period of intense self-doubt. Americans in general have forgotten the luxury of self-righteousness. Because we are not sure of ourselves as a nation and as a society, we listen with a genuine, if tentative, openness to the ideas of others. One good result is that thinking becomes more rational and the thinker more willing to give reasons for his or her ideas and deeds and to measure those reasons against the other person's.

Israelis have been nurtured on the idea that history has proved them right (for they did not perish in the gas chambers) and their achievements have vindicated their commitments (who wants to doubt it?). How stimulating it would be for them to confront serious and sympathetic people who are not sure they are always right! The stifling dogmatism and the perpetual certainty that are second nature in Israeli discourse — and serve to make the opposition look ridiculous — will have to be called into question. I recall trying to argue with an Israeli counterpart on a scholarly matter, until he said to me, "The only important question before us is this: How is it possible for you to err so completely?"

Another contribution American Jews may make is to stimulate questioning of special privilege and special pleading. Ralph Nader's influence has not reached Israel. Consumerism and environmental concerns are just taking root. Meanwhile, bastions of privilege and special preference — *protekzia* — legitimate the rights of a few and violate those of the public at large. To quote Rosenzweig and Tamarin again: "When Israeli statehood came, the leadership had entrenched itself well enough to create by perfectly democratic means an autocratic rule by a socialist bureaucracy."

Pragmatically, it is much better to enjoy the patronage of someone within that bureaucracy than not. In this regard Orthodox Jews are in an enviable position, because they enjoy direct access to the part of the bureaucracy under the control of the "religious" political parties and may therefore win a hearing for their ideas. It goes without saying that American Orthodox Jews have important things to say to the religious sector of Israeli life, particularly concerning the sensible exercise of *its* special privileges.

Orthodox Jews from America bring with them the recognition of a pluralistic and diverse Jewish community. They do not like it and do not wish to maintain it, and that is why they emigrate to the State of

Israel. But they do know that to build a stable society people have to reckon with difference, make compromises, above all learn to work with people with whom they disagree. Israeli life on both right and left, religious and secular, tends to extremes. The gifts of compromise, forbearance, commitment to the common and necessary task — gifts that make American Jewish community life possible — can come, with American Orthodox Jews, to Israeli affairs as well. That is not to say they do come, since the opposite seems to characterize the emigrants. They leave whatever tolerance they learned at home and build, in the wilderness of Judea and Samaria, messianic communes and islands of the saved. But there is more than one form of Orthodoxy, and more than one sort of American Orthodox Jew is at hand. British and American Orthodox Jews who define the ethos of Bar Ilan University, a center of enlightenment and Orthodox outreach, show the other and better way. And they are not few.

Is it possible for immigrants to lead the way to significant changes in the established social, psychological, and cultural patterns of Israeli life? The Iraqi Jews, many of them educated and talented professionals, could not. The German Jews before them were never able to find a place in the ruling elite from which they might have done so. Why should Americans be more successful?

The primary difference among these groups is that American Jewish immigrants left behind a powerful community, on which the State of Israel depends for funds and political support. Between the two groups —

the immigrants and the community at home — a lasting partnership may be created, so that the former gain power and resonance to pierce the resistance of the bureaucracy and its norm-setting, opinion-forming apologists.

Our American friends and relatives in Israel are not beaten people, rejected by the society they have left, as were the German Jews. Nor are they helpless and suddenly impoverished people, dependent upon the established agencies for all preferment, like the Iraqi and Moroccan immigrants. Unlike the Russian Jews, they are not at the mercy of the bureaucracy, and they also are not completely out of touch with the past fifty years in Jewish life. They have not experienced the trauma of life under Soviet communism. They also come to the State of Israel with fewer illusions and high expectations. The Americans are educated people; they have means and come by choice, and they are not inclined to quiver before a bureaucrat. They are taught to "know their rights" — even when they may have none. I see them as our representatives in Israel, our bridge to a society about which we care deeply and which many of us find displeasing in its present aspects. American Jews can bring about considerable change. For what they have, above all, is access to our community and its opinion.

True, Israeli officialdom thinks it can circumvent the masses of the American Jewish community by special dealings with the handful of rich men from whom the bulk of UJA and bond funds come. But the rich still are part of a larger American Jewry. A private visit with an Israeli colonel or a limousine ride with a Jewish agency official cannot in the end outweigh impressions gained from people they understand and respect: Americans like themselves.

Furthermore — and this seems to me even more significant — philanthropy cannot succeed when it is not regarded as philanthropic. It depends, like everything else, upon public acceptance and recognition. The panoply of bond dinners, UJA tours, and federation offices depends for meaning upon the importance accorded these "recognitions" by those who do not enjoy them. If no one will look at your plaque, why put it on the wall? The long-term success of Israeli fund raising, both in bonds and in philanthropy, depends upon the masses' lending importance to the deeds of the upper classes. Once ordinary folk begin to think that these things really do not add up to much, it will be difficult indeed to get those few meaningful gifts, at least in the local communities.

A few years ago, I asked a member of the UJA Young Leadership cabinet, an American who at home spends four days a week on UJA business, "Do you have influence in the State of Israel when you go there?" He replied that he thought he did, for he knows "Golda" and "Moshe" and whoever else there is to know. I said, "In that case, why can you not help to secure for us Conservative Jews the same government support enjoyed by the Orthodox in Israel?" He said, "Oh, of course I have influence, but if I ever tried to tell the Israelis what to do, or asked them why they do what they do, I don't think I'd have influence anymore. Come to think of it, I guess I don't have any anyhow." Now what will happen when this man's friends, cousins, nephews, or own children have settled in Israel? And what will be the case when the letters come back, as they do now, from thirty or forty thousand American Jews who have settled, or from two or three thousand young people in the universities, or from all the others who go for an extended stay, and therefore take seriously what happens there? If those who settle and those who stay home discover one another, they may choose to do together the things that neither can do alone. They can begin to make the distinctively American contribution that Israeli society sorely needs.

4

All Jews—Again

The 1967 war, with its quick and decisive victory, seemed to cost much less than it did. In the messianic euphoria of the next six years, Israelis, as well as American Jews, honestly conceived that "Jewish history" had come to an end. The history of desperation, insecurity, and powerlessness characteristic of the Jewish people for so long was now concluded. A new, "normal" history, the story of confidence, security, control of one's own destiny, had begun. Indeed, 1967 may be called the triumph of the Zionist conception of the State of Israel as the normalization of Jewry, of the effort on the part of the Jewish people to take command of their own destiny, to be exactly as they imagined others to be, in making decisions about their own future. Since, as Samuel said in talmudic times, the sole difference between this age and the world to come is subjugation to the rule of pagans, 1967 marked the beginning of the world to come.

It lasted for six years. Israelis learned in 1973 that they too are Jews, not exempt from the realities of the history of a small, weak, but resilient and resourceful people. That seems to me not a disaster. The Jewish people, after all, have endured for these many centuries by finding a balance between the stubbornness and tenacity, on the one side, and the adaptability and flex-

68   ibility, on the other, required of any people intending to live for eternity. For history goes on and on, and many things happen, not all of them good. The strength of Jewry and its difference from other peoples, many of them now forgotten by all except us, is our will to endure, to do what must be done to go onward. It may seem pointless or hopeless, but it has been our way. I believe, so far as the past tells us anything at all about the future, a hundred or a thousand years from now, if there is a humankind at all, then some tiny segment of humankind will remember us and argue contentiously about "us" and "them," about who is a Jew or what is a Jew.

True, the Israelis have paid a heavy price for the success of 1967. But we American Jews were forced to pay that price too. If they were overconfident and cocksure, we were subservient and craven. If they insisted on doing all the talking, we were content to listen and accept instruction. The price we paid, in the suppression of our good sense and the repression of our natural self-respect, was also paid by the Israelis, those few, at any rate, who cared to talk with us to begin with. For they were deprived of such contribution as we might make. Consider the scandalous hostility addressed to the Hadassah delegation, in 1971. This was because Hadassah would not concede that Zionism consisted solely in ceasing to be a Zionist by settling in the land. The need for *Aliyah* is greater now than it was then yet it is unlikely that diaspora Zionists will be excommunicated for preferring to live abroad and serve, if less materially, yet with a whole heart.

All of us paid dearly in those grim days of October 1973. We believed that Arabs lie, that Israelis tell the truth. But after three days of war, we learned we could not believe anyone. We assumed that Arabs run, but they did not run, and there were no battlefield miracles to raise our hopes to the heights. And all of us imagined that we could perpetually indulge our contentiousness — the Israelis and American Jews alike — and make no decisions, undertake no initiatives.

I think, though, that the truly grievous cost of 1967 lies in the profoundly opposite response to the 1980s. If then we hoped too much, now and afterward we fear too much. If then we saw ourselves at the beginning of the messianic day, today with an equal lack of reality we imagine we face unremitting disaster. Having scaled emotional heights, we find ourselves fallen to the depths of despair.

Let me explain. In 1967 and for a long time afterward, both in the State of Israel and in American Jewry, people thought that Jewish history as the story of powerlessness and suffering had reached a conclusion. The State of Israel had solved the Jewish problem by constituting a free and stable and strong society, in which Jews could secure their safety and live a life without oppression, either material or psychological. That sense of security faded in 1973, in the aftermath of a war that, though successful in many military ways, began with a disaster and nearly ended in catastrophe. So while the ultimate victory retrieved matters, it did not restore the ebullient confidence that had characterized morale since 1967. The 1982 invasion of Lebanon, for its part, ended all notion that with the creation of the State of Israel the Jewish people, in the State of Israel at least, had attained autonomous independence of other nations. The State of Israel turned out to suffer at least as many and as severe limitations on its freedom of action as any other small and inconsequential group, whether nation or ethnic group or religious community. Others decided much. Jews remained dependent. A client-state, a state dependent upon massive foreign support, hardly may claim to have "left history behind" or solved "the Jewish problem" of dependence — and even parasitism. Solutions lay within: in the belief that Jews live freely and contribute not by toleration but by right, wherever human beings live freely and exercise the fundamental human rights of freedom. Israelis then turned out, in the aftermath of the extravagant claims of 1967, to live no more independently and no more freely than any Jews anywhere. So they began to despair.

It is to that widespread despair that I speak: If we choose to be ourselves, the Jewish people, then we have to reassess what it means, and has always meant, to assume the responsibility and the destiny of Jewish "peoplehood." If the experience of the centuries has taught us anything, it has taught us a certain skepticism about pronouncements of salvation and a certain hopefulness in the face of setback. But that lesson does not derive from a wholly this-worldly, essentially tired wisdom. It has come to us, throughout the centuries from A.D. 70 to 1967, through a particular and

distinctive perception of life, of ourselves, and of our
task.

I refer to the tradition of Rabbinic Judaism, which, from the second to the nineteenth centuries, constituted all of normative Judaism and gave definition to heresy and creative challenge and formative symbols to philosophy, theology, and mysticism alike. What is it in the Rabbinic Judaism that proved remarkably congruent to the situation of the Jewish people? At its origins, Rabbinic Judaism came into being in response to the destruction of the Second Temple. Its age of extraordinary creativity followed the still greater disaster of Bar Kokba. That is, the main lines of Rabbinic Judaism were laid down from approximately 70 to approximately 130, and its towering figures and extraordinary achievements were the work of the thirty years from approximately 140 to 170. In other words, nearly 1900 years of Judaism were based upon that single, remarkable century, in which the Jewish people transformed themselves and revised their future (to be sure, in part by rewriting their past).

This is not the right place in which to lay out what I conceive to be the central mythic structure, the primary symbolic modes, of Rabbinic Judaism. It is only to hint that the times call our minds back to the beginnings, because we are at a time of new beginnings. We have had our Holocaust, and, to speak bluntly, we have also had our Bar Kokba. The messianic response to catastrophe — the claim that, in yet a little while, we shall find solace in the denouement of history — has now been proven as inappropriate to the twentieth century as it was to the second century, and for the same reason: Short of atomic war, history does not end, at least not the history of the Jewish people, because of anything frail human beings can accomplish. It was one thing to build again. The creation of the State of Israel in our day was the sign of Jewish stubbornness in the face of ultimate disaster. It is quite another thing to have seen the state as a sign of the end time, not as building a school in the aftermath of the Temple, but as the new Temple itself. That was the intent of Bar Kokba; he meant to recover what was lost — the cult — instead of turning toward the future. The rabbis of the times, by contrast, were determined, not to reconstruct what could not authentically be regained, but to ask what, out of the past, might be used to reshape the people, and their answer (to be all too brief) was to rebuild the Temple through the society of the people, to find in the commonplace life of the villages and streets the new and broader foundations of the sanctuary.

In endowing the Jewish people with the sanctity formerly reserved for the holy place and cult, the rabbis accomplished a revolution that has not yet run its course. And this, I think, is why their remarkable achievement speaks to us now. For just as they made the Jewish people into the sanctuary, so we have once again to renew the conception that we are indeed a people, one people, unlike other peoples in the distinctiveness of our understanding of the meaning of "peoplehood." Just as what we regard as religious differs from what Protestants regard as religious (and vice versa), so what we regard as the meaning of "peoplehood" differs in profound ways from what the other peoples of humankind understand by this concept. No matter: Our problem is ourselves.

These observations are relevant because, at terrible cost, the Israelis now have rejoined the Jewish people. That is, after six years of life as a normal state, from 1967 to 1973, they reentered the situation of Jewry for twenty centuries, that situation which, to begin with, gave birth to Rabbinic Judaism, and with which Rabbinic Judaism proved remarkably congruent. Now that there are no more certainties, now that the future looks unsure, Israelis find themselves in command of a diminished reality, like Jews through the ages. Now they will understand us better, and we them. They will view with sympathy, not contempt, the grotesque, time-serving compromises of the Golus Jews, the capacity for self-doubt and self-criticism, the devotion to the mind and ideas — because these are eternal — instead of to power and glory, which pass. Having denied the *Golah* and thought to reach back to Bar Kokba (and to David), they have once more, not to affirm the *Golah,* but at least to learn its lessons. That is why I believe that the arrogance and self-righteousness of the invincible Israelis of 1967 are done with. People who could condemn hijacking by others but justify it when they did, who could deplore destruction of civilian aircraft in Libya but not in the Sinai, who could shoot people in their beds and call it courageous, brilliant self-defense (but only in Beirut) — such people can do no wrong and exact from their friends total submission. And I think those people are no longer with us. The Israelis of today and tomorrow appreciate their Jewish and gentile friends — with all their flaws — and they know full well that we Jews of America are their friends, because we and they are one.

I think the time of dictating to us is done with, the time of talking with us and even of listening to us is about to begin. An unreal relationship, based upon a much larger, still more fantastic conception of themselves, is a bad memory. For our part, the way forward lies in constructive exchanges of ideas, not recriminations (from abroad) or complaints (when in the land itself). To move forward, to begin with, we have to find out what we are talking about, to make the contribution of fair-minded and objective commentary only when we have mastered the text.

American Jews include an amazing group of talented people. We have mastered the many torahs of living modern society, and the torah of building a fair and open way of life. Now that the Israelis know that self-indulgence, favoritism, *protekzia,* contentiousness, indifference to others, ultimately affect even the efficiency of the army, they are apt to want to learn how other people build a society, conduct a democracy, and construct a way of life responsive to the rights and ideas of the other person. They and we have paid a bitter price, but it can, in the long view, turn out to have been an investment in the accurate perception of reality.

Part Three
Issues in Black, White, and Jewish

Journey to a Nightmare:
The South African Connection

I do not pretend to know a great deal more about South Africa than you learn from reading newspapers. But in one respect I have something to say that you cannot learn from the press — what it is like to be there. What do you learn about the world and about yourself on a voyage to another time and another place?

When I arrived in South Africa in May 1976 to address the Jewish Community of the Republic, I had every intention of talking only about Jewish things, the inner life of the people, the state of Judaic belief, and similar matters. That intention proved to be a gross error. I had the notion that Jewish concerns and human concerns of Jews could be kept separate. I imagined that a Jewish community could make its life within a mental wall, so that the context of the Jewish community would play no role in the inner life of the community.

The first difference from American experience I observed in Johannesburg Jewry was that the people listen with great respect to authority, which, in this case, meant me. When I spoke to about one thousand people on my second night in the Republic, I had the eerie feeling that no one in the room was breathing, so dense was the silence.

The second difference I observed as I visited various schools, met with boards of directors of social agencies and community institutions, was that a totally authoritarian philosophy of education and public life permeates the Jewish community. In schools students are taught essentially to respect the teacher and to memorize what he or she says. (In passing, I may say that I brought up the subject of women's liberation and met nothing but hostility.) The notion that education is gained through free inquiry is wholly lacking and perceived as frightening.

The third difference I found is that I had to be careful about what I said in offices and on the telephone. The Transvaal is certainly the most tense part of the Republic. I was told by people who knew what they were talking about that the telephones in the offices of the Board of Deputies are bugged. These people also took for granted that the security police are well informed about what is said in the office themselves. I should assume that mail is opened and read.

I had already learned that the South African Broadcasting Corporation (SABC) staff is anti-Semitic. I was scheduled for an interview on a popular rush-hour program, and the interviewer told me beforehand not to mention that I was to speak on mainly Jewish topics, because no one wanted to hear about such things. Instead I was asked during the interview whether I thought the World Council of Churches should give arms to "terrorists" in the North, and what I thought

of the international communist conspiracy against
Christianity. That SABC also broadcasts sermons on
the protocols of the elders of Zion and the international Jewish conspiracy, but suppresses broadcasts in
the "World at War" series that deal with the destruction of European Jewry. I was told, on good authority,
that an anti-Semitic, Nazi group enjoys powerful friends
within the government. For example, when the Board
of Deputies informed the government of the activities
of Nazis in the Republic, within twenty-four hours
copies of the correspondence were delivered to the
Nazis mentioned therein. This brief catalog should give
you some notion of the human environment that
greeted me within a few days of my arrival.

Let me generalize the world defined by these facts.
What I found was that in order to maintain an authoritarian state, in order to preserve white supremacy in
politics, culture, economics, and all other spheres of
human life, the whites themselves have to submit to
considerable limitations upon the normal modes of
human free choice and expression. And among the
whites, the Jews have to make a trade: They may accept the position of a barely tolerated, insecure, but
useful minority, along with the extraordinarily comfortable, material benefits enjoyed by South African
whites in general. But in exchange for this toleration,
they among all whites must accept the psychological
norms of the country: submission to authority and
surrender of personal freedom of expression. For
South Africa is a place in which for the expression of
opinion, for hearing a proscribed idea, you can be

thrown into prison or ostracized by the community. The jails hold people whose crime is to have printed a leaflet or given a speech deemed "communist." The result of this exchange of a measure of freedom for a measure of security and a large helping of material comfort is the diminution of freedom. That sounds like a fair, if fearful and cowardly, trade. But when you consider the result of nonfreedom in educational and cultural life quite remote from the issues about which one must be careful, you realize that there is no boundary to censorship. Self-censorship is best of all, of course, and that takes the form of people settling for an amiable status quo. How do you transmit the subtle disciplines of self-censorship, if not by educating children in such a way that they learn to censor themselves and conform to authority in matters that do not count? How do you establish a stable situation of material wealth and human spiritual deprivation, if not by organizing all sorts of institutions in such a way as to reinforce the common, secular norm?

As the days in Johannesburg passed I found myself ever more sensitive to the climate of repression. I had to watch my words in public, by phone, even in offices. I was made aware of deep anti-Semitism by the white population in general. Hatred and fear are indivisible. People who hate and fear one group are apt to hate and fear a great many groups. The Jews are perceived and tend to perceive themselves essentially as resident aliens. And why not, since the foundation stone of the white minority's policy of separate development of the races is that the blacks in white areas are resident aliens? If the blacks, born for generations in Soweto, still cannot (as of the time of my visit) own their own homes and enjoy the right of residence and free movement, if they are viewed as people with no stake whatsoever in the life of the Republic but as guest workers from a foreign land in the bush, why should not other groups, not only the Jews, also be perceived as essentially alien and outside? Since no one among the whites assumes the blacks are loyal to the Republic, why should anyone take for granted the trustworthiness and loyalty of any other group?

Potchefstroom University is Judenrein — "pure of Jews" — a Nazi word used in the Nazi sense, because a condition of employment is that the professor profess Christianity. I was brought to the office of the university's chief fund-raiser, who had invited me to admire the university's buildings and to encourage "the rich Jews" of Johannesburg to build more of them. He had assembled diverse faculty members to talk with me. The first question was, "Don't you think that Israel, America, and South Africa should unite in common cause against international communism? Don't you agree that there is an international conspiracy against God, a conspiracy formed of the enemies of America, Israel, and South Africa alike?" My answer was in two parts. "First, I have to tell you, I am an American and cannot discuss or advocate the foreign policy of the State of Israel. Second, if you want a defense of American policy in Angola or in southern Africa in general, we have to begin with the notion that we have no vested interest in your system, and we abhor it. We can and do conduct business with black states and find nothing menacing or even incongruous therein. Simonstown and your strategic position on the oil routes can be safeguarded for us in more than one way. And who knows who conspires against God?" I have to admit that it was not a long or productive discussion. In fact, the people gulped down their tea and left within twenty minutes of my arrival. For my part, I left as soon as I could. I refused, thereafter, to lecture at any other Afrikaans-speaking university. My hosts did not blame me.

That night, back in Johannesburg, we attended the musical *Ipi Tombi,* which was entirely performed by blacks. Here on the stage before me were people of exceptional talent who could convey the flavor of their culture through dance and music, even to people who could not speak their language. Outside, in front of the theater, was a line of cars to take the performers back to their homes in the black townships, since there were no means of transport for blacks and they could not take buses or trains reserved for whites. The great singers and dancers before me stood for the blacks who are not great singers and dancers, but who are simple working people. They are drawn out of the tribal life, out of the bush, to turn the wheels of white industry. They then had no unions. They cannot negotiate the price of their service. They cannot own their homes. They reside on the fringes of the white cities only on condition that they are suitably employed, and that their employer so certifies. Their homes lack the sim-

plest amenities — water, electricity, plumbing. They
have little money for food, they dress their children in
rags, as best they can; they survive as best they can.
They are aliens in a land to which they, as much as the
whites, have a valid claim of residence and development. They build the country, dig its mines, run its
industries, till its fields. But they have no share in the
fruits of their labor, no share in the common polity,
no right not accorded to them by the grace of the
white minority. When, in speeches around the country,
I referred to these facts, I was told that, after all, they
are better off than they were in the bush, that their
standard of living is higher than that of blacks in other
parts of Africa.

The things I learned about the country are things
you all know. What I learned about myself is that freedom is indivisible. If I am not free, you are not free,
and if you are not free, I cannot have freedom either.
What happens to the other person happens to me, not
in some deep, philosophical sense, but in a very concrete and immediate way. If to keep the blacks down,
their freedom must be taken away, then a condition
of the system will be that my freedom must also be
diminished. And there is no dividing freedom. If I cannot say some things without fear of the security police,
I cannot say anything at all without fear. If I have to
avoid saying some things, I have to avoid thinking them
also. If I have to deny myself, then my own condition
is a situation of unfreedom.

It may be a more materially comfortable situation.

From the handsome suburbs of Cape Town you can see, at the center of the harbor, Robben Island, where political prisoners are put away. But the island is no less free than the mainland. You cannot see the people on the island. But they are there, and you know why they are there. And if you want to stay where you are, in a large house, with three or four house "boys" and nannies, if you want to sit at your dining table and ring a bell so that the serving woman, wearing white gloves to avoid contact with your food, will take away one course and bring the next, if you want to enjoy the privilege of never sleeping under the same roof with a person of another color and of keeping your servants in little doghouses by the side, or on top, of your house — if you want all these wonderful prerequisites of the good life, then you'd better shut up and take what's yours and forget the other fellow.

What I learned about being Jewish is that there are no lines of division, no unmarked boundaries, between my being Jewish and my being human. The one flows into the other and back again. That is why I found Auschwitz in Potchefstroom. There I found, too, what it must have been like to be a Christian in Nazi Germany. Time and again my thoughts went to Dietrich Bonhoeffer, a Christian theologian in Hitler's time, who was hanged by the Nazis for his dissent. I realized the courage he showed in taking upon himself a burden that he could have left for others, in seeing himself among the oppressed, even though he could have joined the oppressors, or, being moral, at least stood idly by. So in South Africa I found myself a Christian, a black, a Jew, a person of the West, an American — a human being made up of all these things.

We are not talking about a situation that can be ignored. Human beings are suffering. That they have suffered for centuries does not make their suffering any less pressing. The situation is urgent because suffering and oppression always are now, always happen when they happen, however long they already have happened. We cannot stand idly by. We must make the state of South African conditions a matter of personal engagement and personal concern, just as we must make the condition of humanity in any country, of human oppression, whether in Africa, India, China, or the Soviet Union, a matter of our own engagement. For if people in those and other countries are not free, then we cannot be free. The frontiers of freedom encompass the whole of humanity. What I learned in South Africa is that we really are our brothers' and sisters' keepers, and that our brothers and our sisters are everyone.

Blacks and Jews:
Postscript to a Nightmare

Both Jews and blacks frame their understanding of themselves by invoking a single story: Israel in the promised land. For the blacks one reaches freedom "over Jordan." "Israel in Egyptland" is the black in America. Jews of course know *Israel* as the Land of Israel, the promised land, the land and state we Jews have created in our own century. Israel has an embassy in Cairo, so much for Israel in Egyptland. So nothing could be more the same, and nothing could be more different.

So too, Jews and blacks understand themselves in the dark and gloom of nightmare. Blacks remember slavery and today look on a world that sees them as different. They find it hard to make their way as a minority in a world of whites. Jews remember centuries of suffering and themselves survived the murder of the Jews of Europe. Today they too make their way in a world that sees them as different — not really normal or ordinary. And there is always dislike of the unlike. That is why some blacks and some Jews find life easier among their own kind. Despite the differences, nothing could be more the same than the world in which both Jews and blacks must make their lives.

No wonder then that each group sees the other in a way in which it does not see third parties: "*They* know what it's like, so they should understand." Nor is it surprising that the world beyond perceives the two groups in much the same way, though for different reasons. To both are extended the occasional courtesies of toleration of difference, and both receive, each in its own manner and measure, the witless gifts of condescension. Jews and blacks seek dignity, demand the right to be what they wish when they wish. For the Jews it means to be Jewish when they want, and to be individuals, part of undifferentiated humanity, when they want. For blacks it means at times equality and at times special access, at times the right to be racially differentiated and at times to be part of a colorblind and neutral society. These contradictory demands accurately portray the contradictions and tensions that make interesting the lives of Jews and blacks alike.

For Jews the nightmare of America is Hitler, who can come as a demagogue to persuade other Americans that all their problems come from the Jews, and all they have to do is get rid of the Jews. For Jews, therefore, whatever hints at anti-Semitism in broad daylight sounds the alarm of a midnight nightmare. Quotas for one group mean exclusion of another, for when so many places are reserved for someone by reason of traits not defined by the task at hand, then none can qualify except by race or its equivalent. To Jews who recall the history of the past two hundred years, quotas mean exclusion of Jews — not in Poland and Germany alone, but by Harvard and Columbia as well. For Jews the dream of the age is the creation of the State of Israel, refuge and hope for the Jewish people everywhere. Insecure at home and witnessing the thirty-year war against the Jewish state, Jews take most seriously any threat, verbal or material, to the standing of that state.

In light of these two nightmares, the Democratic primary campaign of 1984 framed a long, dark night. The black candidate, perceived as a hero by blacks, to many Jews appeared a demagogue, a friend of the enemies of the State of Israel, associate of anti-Semites, himself an anti-Semite.

For blacks the nightmare of America today is exclusion, the indifference of the many to the longtime suffering of the few, the hostility of the many to the naked human needs of the few. Blacks look out on a community still paying the price of slavery, living in less than equal housing, working in less than equal jobs, going to strife-ridden schools and coming home to crime-ridden streets, to broken families and drug-afflicted, sick children. They do not count many years backward to an age in which in every aspect of their lives they were a persecuted caste, treated with brutality. Now they ask only to be recognized as a protected caste, assisted to overcome the long-term effects of centuries of brutality.

Programs in affirmative action on behalf of blacks (and others of their status and history) merely take up the problems of exclusion and degradation inflicted by more substantial and far older programs of negative action. Identifying, moreover, with others they perceive (fairly or unfairly) to be their counterparts, some blacks, particularly younger ones, see as powerful and not always beneficent that same Jewish state that Jews, old and young, perceive as a beacon of hope and pride.

In competition and in conflict, therefore, blacks and Jews faced off in the 1984 Democratic primaries, and the long-term results have not yet fully emerged. We do not now know whether the established alliance, built on both shared needs and deep sympathies over a century past, has broken down. What we do know is that neither group wishes to go it alone, without the support of friends in the other group . As many Jewish and black leaders already have counseled, we have to look forward and not backward. For the recent past in 1984 for Jews proved a nightmare for exactly the reasons that for blacks it was a time of dreaming. But now in the full light of day in 1985 we know that a nightmare is just that, a dream of no consequence we do not chose to give it.

Some issues demand attention in a different frame of discourse, because they are not particular to Jews and to blacks. Numerous economic questions, matters of public and social policy, affecting all Americans equally, demand attention in a different setting from the one in which Jews speak as Jews to blacks listening as blacks, and in which blacks respond with "we" to the Jewish "you" or "they." Jews and blacks have the right to be something else, many other things, and for both groups life adds up to more than issues framed in the present confrontation.

To begin to isolate issues demanding attention in the context of interchange between Jews and blacks, we shall speak of two alone, one a symbolic point important to Jews, the other a symbolic point important to blacks. In isolating two central symbolic matters, recognizing the weight and depth of what they represent, we point to possible approaches suitable to numerous other issues that, in due course, will demand exposure and analysis. Blacks speak of affirmative action, Jews speak of support for the State of Israel. Blacks resent Jews' opposition to affirmative action, which many call quotas. Jews profoundly resent blacks' espousal of the Arab cause aiming at the destruction of the State of Israel.

As soon as we phrase matters in this way we fall into error. For not all blacks share the hostility of some toward the State of Israel. Jews strongly favor equality of access, including programs to make meaningful such equality. The very framing of the symbols of dispute obscures matters, establishing solid blocs instead of fluid ones, fixing as permanent attitudes of the moment and irritations that will pass.

It is not as if we can say to the two parties, "You trade Israel for affirmative action," that is, each side gives up something in favor of what the other side wants most. Life does not permit easy trade-offs. And who are we — intellectuals, people who read books and write articles — to offer a trade, since no one has appointed us to speak on behalf of our disputing commu-

92   nities? A different way forward demands exploration.

On the one side, Jews have to reconsider whether opposition to affirmative action defines their principal position. The statements of Jewish organizations engaged in the matter show that it need not. Jewish organizations clearly favor programs to open doors and also to make it possible for blacks themselves to open and to walk through those doors. That aspect of the Jewish community's position demands emphasis. Jewish organizations should concentrate on framing a constructive approach to securing for blacks access to positions they want and making certain that blacks get and retain those positions. Quotas raise legitimate fears, not only among Jews. Therefore alternative paths to the same destination require discovery.

But let us be clear on what that destination is: We Jews do favor a free society, in which all Americans not only have the right to hold any position for which they are qualified but also have every reason to expect to get and keep such positions. We Jews do favor cities in which anyone can live wherever that person chooses, schools in which young people of diverse origin study together, integration when people wish to integrate, autonomy when people wish to be by themselves.

On the other side, blacks have to recast their view of foreign affairs in such a way that wins the confidence of friends of the State of Israel (including, I repeat, large numbers of blacks). Specifically, where there is legitimate criticism of Israeli foreign or domestic policy, let us hear it. But the very existence of the State of Israel cannot be advanced as a topic for legitimate debate — not here, not now, and not with us.

We shall happily discuss that issue when it is equally legitimate to discuss whether or not the United States of America should revert to the status of a British colony (or a mandate, which was the status of Palestine before the State of Israel came into being), or whether or not the Soviet Union should return to China and Iran the vast tracts of land the Russian imperialists acquired in the nineteenth century. Nor shall we fail to mention giving independence to Latvia, Lithuania, and Estonia, perhaps also to the Ukraine and White Russia, and restoring Bessarabia to Romania. The list of such topics is not a short one. Among them, of course, we can include assigning New Mexico, Arizona, and California to Mexico, and miles of upstate New York to the Iroquois nation.

On the other hand, within the framework of fair-minded discussion of other countries and their policies, the State of Israel should be subject to criticism — in this same, projected discussion — along the same lines that guide criticism of other countries of the first, second, third, and fourth worlds. True, Israel trades with South Africa, but hardly so much as Nigeria, not to mention Mozambique and the other countries of sub-Saharan Africa.

Above all, blacks cannot condone or tolerate bigotry when it affects the Jews and object only when it reaches the blacks. But blacks are not alone in bearing responsibility to reject all forms of racism, including

94   anti-Semitism. The presidential campaign of 1984 will not be soon forgotten. The fears it brought to life will pass only when the long-term allies, blacks and Jews together, on terms of complete equality, agree that no form of bigotry is less intolerable than any other.

At the same time, the blacks can help the Jewish community by giving an example of how legitimate public discourse on Israeli and other Middle Eastern questions should go forward. Specifically, they can provide a model for Jews as well as other Americans of how critical, constructive discourse on all aspects of Middle Eastern policy may proceed in a fair and balanced manner. At this time, in the organized Jewish community, that kind of discussion takes place solely within rigid and narrow constraints — so long as no one is listening. The reason is fear that, in a time of danger, we do not wish to appear to be giving aid to the enemy. But that fear has now become so extreme that a negative comment on one aspect of Israeli policy or society constitutes an affirmation of the entire position of anti-Semitism, on the one side, or of the PLO and other "rejectionists," on the other. A criticism in the context of criticism of other nations in general, a comment in the setting of an affirmative and fair-minded discussion — these can only set a worthwhile example. Blacks have their fears, Jews have theirs, and each can help the other overcome the burden of nightmare.

Part Four
American Jewry at Home

Assimilation and Self-hatred

The word *assimilation* denotes the reception of aliens
by a host society and the aliens' gradual acceptance
of the traits of that host culture. The history of the
Jewish people is the story of how the Jews entered
into one culture after another, and came to regard their
cultural acquisitions as essentially Jewish. Eastern
European cuisine among American Jewry is one obvious example; Greek philosophy among Spanish
Jewry is another; Roman methods of legal codifica-
tion among Palestinian Jewry is a third. In all three
instances Jews took over and Judaized traits derived
from other cultures, and thereafter defended and cher-
ished them as quintessentially Jewish. So we have
stuffed derma, Maimonides, and the Mishnah, to name
three examples of the assimilation through Judaization
of originally alien traits or creations.

The extent of the Jews' assimilation of the various
cultures encountered in their history cannot be over-
estimated. We may not take for granted that we may
find peculiarly "Jewish" approaches to intellectual
life, for example. Some people suppose that the talmudic dialectic is uniquely Jewish. The dialectic, however, is formed of Roman principles of legal codifica-
tion and Greek principles of rhetoric. Perhaps one
might find parallels among contemporary Syriac, late

Babylonian, and Hellenistic traditions, if these were sufficiently well known to us. The Jewish academies of late antiquity certainly are similar in important ways to the Christian monasteries of the same time and place. Although a discipline may be peculiar to a tradition of learning and still be derivative, I doubt that Jewish learning can be associated over a long period of time with any particular discipline. The Jews can lay no persuasive claim to exclusive possession of subtlety or cleverness, devotion to the intellectual life, dedication to matters of the spirit, or any of the other traits, pejorative or complimentary, claimed for them by their religious and secular enemies or apologists.

In the early days of Reform Judaism, it was thought that if we uncover the "origin" of a practice or belief, we may then decide whether it is "essential" or peripheral. Nowadays we see less interest in questions of origins. The exposure of the genetic fallacy may have been part of the reason for this shift. We recognize that determination of the origin does not exhaust the meanings of beliefs or practices. Yet there is another reason for this dwindling of interest. It has become progressively more difficult, with the advance of scholarship, to discover any deeply "Jewish" or "Judaic" practice that was not in some degree the creation of another culture or civilization.

The Jewish calendar, that "unique" construction of Judaism, derives mostly from the Canaanites. One may argue that the festivals were "monotheized" or "Judaized." But, in fact, different verbal explanations have been imposed on the same festivals celebrating the same natural phenomena of the same Palestinian agricultural year. The Jews, over long centuries, have assumed as their own what was produced originally by others. Their infinite adaptability has been made possible by short memories and by tenacious insistence on the Jewish origins of purely gentile or pagan customs. Regardless of whether something was or was not Jewish, a great many things have *become* so. Jewishness thus is not static but dynamic, and assimilation is the source of the dynamism.

It is clear, therefore, that the history of Judaism is also the history of the assimilation by the Jews of the cultural, social, and religious traits characteristic of their neighbors. How shall we evaluate that phenomenon? Here I advance the view of Gerson D. Cohen, presented in a speech at the Boston Hebrew College.

A frank appraisal of the periods of great Jewish creativity will indicate that not only did a certain amount of assimilation and acculturation not impede Jewish continuity and creation, but that, in a profound sense, this assimilation or acculturation was even a stimulus to original thinking and expression and, consequently, a source of renewed vitality. To a considerable degree the Jews survived as a vital group . . . because they changed their names, their language, their clothing, and with them, some of their patterns of thought and expression. This ability to translate, to readapt and reorient themselves to new situations, while retaining a basic inner core of continuity, was largely responsible, if not for their survival, at least for their vitality.

Cohen points out, to be sure, that people on the fringe preferred to identify with the majority group. This occasionally happened. But, Cohen stresses,

We Jews have always been and will doubtless continue to be a minority group. Now a minority that does not wish to ghettoize itself, one that refuses to become fossilized, will inevitably have to acculturate itself, i.e., to assimilate at least to some extent.

Assimilation is a fact of Jewish life and, on the whole, it has been a fact Jews may accept with optimism.

As Cohen stresses, Jews confront the problem of assimilation in two ways. One is to withdraw. The other is to find through assimilation a new source of vitality. Cohen cites Ahad HaAm, who distinguished between *hiqqui shel hitharut* and *hiqqui shel hitbolelut* — imitation stimulated by the challenge of new ideas and imitation motivated by the desire to be absorbed. Cohen advances this notion:

> I would . . . rather speak of the healthy appropriation of new forms and ideas for the sake of our own growth and enrichment. Assimilation . . . can become a kind of blessing, for assimilation bears within it a certain seminal power, which serves as a challenge and a goad to renewed creativity. The great ages of Jewish creativity . . . have always been products of the challenge of assimilation and of the response of leaders, who were to a certain extent assimilated themselves.

Following Cohen, Jews need not regard the assimilation of Jewry into Western civilization as disheartening or threatening. They ought, rather, to see it as invigorating and challenging.

Nor should one suppose that the State of Israel is

exempt from the assimilative condition of diaspora Jewry. Israel uses Hebrew to farm in the modern mode, to manufacture for the world market, to think in a wholly contemporary fashion about the great issues facing modern man, to make war according to the requirements of modern technology. Israeli Jews do not differ from Western Jews; both have adopted the international culture — music, art, literature, philosophy — of Western Europe and North America. There is no place to hide from the transistor radio. No one wants to "escape" from modern medicine. No ghetto is immune from the healthy virus of modernity.

Let us now turn to one of the unwanted consequences of the movement of Jewry from an isolated culture into international civilization. In the past, the Jews were well insulated from the opinions of Gentiles. Their social setting tended to separate them, and their theological conviction rendered them indifferent to what the Gentiles had to say about them. Jews not only knew they were different from others, but also regarded these differences as a matter of destiny. The statement in the *Alenu* prayer, "Who has not made us like Gentiles," was a matter of thanksgiving, pride, and joy, a self-conscious articulation of Israel's status as a unique people. The myth of Jews as a distinct people transformed difference into destiny.

In modern times, assimilation, formerly unconscious and unplanned, became both a public program and a personal policy. The Jews determined that they should live not only among Gentiles but also with them. They would share their way of living, their cultural, social, and economic life and values. In one respect only would they differ: in matters of religion, meaning chiefly questions of faith — and these were not important. This reversal of traditional attitudes was espoused not only by Reform Judaism in Germany but also by modern Orthodox leaders such as Samson R. Hirsch, who taught that Jews could be both good Germans and strictly traditional Jews, read both Goethe and the Talmud. Orthodoxy differed from Reform in its order of priorities: The Torah would stand as the criterion of modernity, and not the reverse.

But before Jews, whether Reform or Orthodox, could conceive of themselves in such a new situation, they had to affirm modern culture in a way in which they had never accepted or affirmed the cultures of ancient and medieval times. The assimilation of ancient and medieval cultures had come about naturally and quietly. It had not challenged the beliefs and practices Jews regarded as eternal and unchanging, but had allowed those beliefs and practices to continue with renewed vigor. Modern assimilation, by contrast, held as a deliberate and positive goal the de-Judaization of the Jews. Supporters of assimilation did not want Jews to become more similar to other citizens in ways not critical to their Jewish identification. Rather, they wanted Jews to stop being Jews at all. The program of assimilationism consisted in the claim that if the nations accepted the Jews as citizens, Jews would stop being so different in so many ways. Further, they would cease to be Jews at all, giving up their distinctive traits as a social group, even abandoning their religion

altogether. It was not a benign program. It was a malign
program in benign disguise.

Now, for the first time in centuries, Jews took to heart what Gentiles said about them. And since the European Jews lived in an age of virulent anti-Semitism, most of what Gentiles had to say was derogatory. The political right regarded the Jews as agents of change and thereafter hated them; the left differed — it hated only what was *Jewish* about the Jews. Liberals argued that allowing Jews to enter into the common life of European politics and culture would hasten their de-Judaization. So the Jewish problem resolved itself into a debate on how to rid Europe of Jews and Judaism.

One result of this debate was the Zionist movement, which accepted the premises of European anti-Semitism, and held that the only solution to the Jewish problem was the creation of a Jewish state, which would "normalize" the character of the Jewish people. That is, Zionism proposed to make the Jews like the Gentiles. Another result was Reform Judaism, which also accepted the premises of European anti-Semitism, and held that the only solution was to limit the differences between Jews and Gentiles to matters of religious belief. Reforming Jewish tradition would permit Jews to become more like their neighbors. Individual Jews reacted in still a third way — and it was profoundly tragic. They responded to the hatred of Gentiles by hating themselves as Jews, by hating those traits the Gentiles thought to be peculiarly Jewish.

European Jewish self-hatred was pathological, producing psychosis and occasionally leading to suicide. But by and large this sickness remained outside Jewish institutions and leadership, for those infected by self-hatred fled the Jewish community. The most profound analysis of the self-hatred of European Jewry is found in Theodor Lessing's *Der jüdische Selbsthass* (Berlin, 1930). Lessing stresses that the Jews of Europe wonder, "Why does no one love us?" And they answer, "Because we are at fault." Lessing sees this as a contemporary psychological counterpart to the traditional theology of disaster: "Because of our sins, we have been exiled from our land." Lessing himself was a sad man who lived a life of self-hatred. He was murdered on August 31, 1933, in Marienbad, by three Sudeten German-Czech Nazis who were paid eighty thousand marks for the deed by Göring (*Der Spiegel,* June 22, 1980, pp. 150–152).

Lessing tells the story of six European Jewish intellectuals, most of whom ended as suicides. One wrote as follows:

> I force myself not to think about it. But what does it help? It thinks within me, it thinks of itself, it does not ask about my wish and will and the natural urge to flee from what is painful, ugly, deadly. It is there, all the time, it is within me: this knowledge about my descent. Just as a leper or a person sick with cancer carries his repulsive disease hidden under his dress and yet knows about it himself every moment, so I carry the shame and disgrace, the metaphysical guilt of my being a Jew.
>
> What are all the sufferings and disappointments and inhibitions that come from outside in comparison with this hell within? To have to be what one despises! . . . Because here

all rationalizations, all attempts to cover up, all desire to lie to oneself, all this is useless here. It is quite clear to me, ruthlessly clear: Jewishness lies in existence. You cannot shake it off. Just as little as a dog or a pig can shake off its being a dog or its being a pig, just so little do I tear myself, my own self, away from the eternal ties of existence, which hold me on that step between man and animal: the Jews.

The closing passage is without parallel even in the pathological literature of Jewish self-hatred.

There exists today hardly a more tragic fate than that of those few who have truly fought themselves free from their Jewish ancestry and who now discover that people do not believe them, do not want to believe them. Where, where can we go? Behind us lie revulsion and disgust, in from of us yawns an abyss. . . . Nameless, rootless. Mercilessly exiled into a circle of hatred rigid with death . . . And I feel as if I had to carry on my shoulders the entire accumulated guilt of that cursed breed of men whose poisonous self-blood is becoming my virus. I feel as if I, I alone, had to do penance for every crime those people are committing against Germanness. . . .

And to the Germans I should like to shout: Remain hard! Remain hard! Have no mercy! Not even with me!

Germans, your walls must remain secure against penetration. They must not have any secret little door in the rear that could be opened for single persons. Because, surely, some day through this little door treason would creep in. . . . Close your hearts and your ears to all those who from out there still beg for admission. Everything is at stake! You last little fortress of Aryanism, remain strong and faithful!

No, no, no — it was not just that God wanted to spare Sodom and Gomorrah because of one righteous man! Not even for the sake of ten, not for the sake of a hundred righteous men.

Away with this pestilential poor! Burn out this nest of wasps! Even though along with the unrighteous a hundred righteous ones are destroyed. What do they matter? What do we matter? What do I matter? No! Have no mercy! I beg of you (Translated by Horst R. Moehring).

Self-hatred is not unique to the Jews. It is an element in every human personality. All people fight the conflict between self-esteem and self-hatred. Self-esteem begins in earliest childhood. In *Childhood and Society* (New York, 1950), Erik Erikson writes, "Through the coincidence of physical mastery and cultural meaning, of functional pleasure and social recognition, one achieves a realistic self-esteem." The child naturally begins with self-love, but it must be corroborated by experience that gives the child the feeling that he fulfills his own ego ideal. Erikson stresses that there must be tangible social recognition, "a feeling of continued communal meaning," in order for the adolescent to develop a mature sense of self-esteem.

Let us come to our own day. The Jewish child in Europe and in North America faces discontinuity between what he or she learns in childhood and at home, on the one side, and continued communal meaning, on the other. At home children learn that they are Jews. What they learn about the meaning of that fact will vary. In some few homes, being Jewish is a source of joy and endless pleasures; in many others, it is merely a social datum. Yet the mere fact of Jewishness contains within itself no pleasures or joys, no larger meaning, nothing of communal or theological significance.

This fact contradicts a communal fact that the child perceives quite early: Not everyone is Jewish. Most

people are something else. The child rapidly senses
that being Jewish is being "different." Being Jewish,
therefore, may stand as an obstacle to the child's
growth. The cultural meaning of the home may conflict with the social recognition achieved outside the
home. The Jewish child's self-love may *not* be corroborated by experience — for the child cannot expect
an opportunity to employ what he or she learns in
the Jewish experiences of childhood and to acquire
thereby a feeling of continued communal meaning.

After Jewish children become aware that they are
different, they also must listen while the gentile world
openly or insidiously tells them the "Jewish difference" is a bad one. The majority is not only different,
but better — for, after all, the world celebrates Christ-
mas, but only some Jews celebrate Hanukah. The psychological consequences, in terms of Erikson's analysis,
will be obvious. Jewish children will sense a deep discontinuity, and will see themselves as inferior, different, and bad because of the difference. If the Jewish
child attends a public school, this awareness cannot be
postponed beyond the second or third grade, a period
in which the earliest psychological conflicts are by and
large dormant. According to Erikson, at that age the
children may continue to compare themselves with
their parents; this comparison may arouse a sense of
guilt and of inferiority. Now for the boy the religion
of the father enters the picture: The family is Jewish.
Being Jewish is being different. Being Jewish is not as
good as being Gentile. The father, toward whom guilt
is already present, is Jewish and made the child. The

normal guilt of the earliest school years may thus turn into hatred of the father — or it may produce hatred of the self in place of hatred of the father.

Let us bring together the two approaches to the problem of Jewish self-hatred. Lessing tells us that the culture and religion of the Jews taught them over the centuries to blame themselves for their own misfortunes. Erikson tells us that the personality development of each child is apt to be accompanied by severe psychological problems if self-esteem cannot be fully established in the earliest years through communal as well as familial support. Jewish children in the Western communities experience being a minority and being different from people one admires. The response is cultural and historical, on the one side, and psychological and personal on the other. And the inevitable union of history and culture with psychology and personality development cannot be postponed; the one supplies explanations for the experiences produced by the other.

If we look for pathological cases of Jewish self-hatred among North American Jewry, we should easily find them. But on the whole, self-hatred takes a different form here. It is merely neurotic, not psychotic as in Lessing's cases, and it is not limited to individuals. It characterizes the community as a whole, It is reflected in the Jewish community's commitment to nonsectarianism, and in the community's limited support for the cultural, scholarly, and religious programs and institutions that make Jews Jewish.

How do we account for the difference? I think the

obvious answer is that on the whole Jews in the United
States and Canada enjoy an enviable status in economic, social, cultural, and political life. Anti-Semitism does not take the virulent and destructive forms
it did in Western Europe before World War II. We have
no anti-Semitic political parties; universities are, on the
whole, open to Jews; most professions accept Jews;
discrimination in the executive suite and in upper-class
social clubs by and large constitutes a form of social
snobbery, not an ideology of race and culture. American and Canadian societies in the balance are not
racist. But these facts cannot change the situation of
the *Galut:* The Jews are still a minority, still correctly
see themselves as different from the majority. Those
differences still add up to abnormality.

Why are Jews in the United States and Canada in the
forefront of universal causes, to the exclusion of their
own interest and identity? Charles Liebman, writing
in the journal *The Religious Situation 1969,* examines
the reasons often given for this phenomenon. He rejects
the notion that Jewish liberalism, cosmopolitanism,
and internationalism rest on "traditional" Jewish values, for, as he points out, it is the secular not the religious Jew who espouses cosmopolitanism. Jewish
religious values, in fact, are folk oriented rather than
universalistic.

He similarly rejects the view that the Jews' social
status, which is not commensurate with their economic
attainments, accounts for their attraction to the fringes
of politics. This theory accounts, Liebman says, for
Jewish radicalism rather than Jewish liberalism.

Further, Jewish radicals, a small element of the community, normally abandon Jewish community life; the liberals dominate it.

A third explanation derives from the facts of history: Liberal parties supported the emancipation of the Jews; conservative parties opposed it. But this was not the case in the United States. Indeed. until the New Deal, Jews tended to be Republican, not Democratic or Socialist.

Liebman posits that the appeal of liberalism is strongest among Jews estranged from the religious tradition. This appeal, he says, "lies in the search for a universalistic ethic to which a Jew can adhere *but* which is seemingly irrelevant to specific Jewish concerns and, unlike radical socialism, does not demand total commitment at the expense of all other values."

Since the emancipation, Jews have constantly driven to free themselves from the condition that Judaism thrusts on them. Liebman writes: "The impetus for intellectual and religious reform among Jews, the adoption of new ideologies and life styles, but above all else the changing self-perception by the Jew of himself and his condition was not simply a desire to find amelioration from the physical oppression of the ghetto. It was rather a desire for emancipation from the very essence of the Jewish condition."

Jews brought the ideals of universal humanism and cosmopolitanism home to the community so that Jewish difference was played down. Look, for example, at the *Union Prayerbook,* and count the number of times the congregation prays for "all mankind." The

New Liberal Prayerbook in England so emphasizes the
universal to the exclusion of the particular that one
might write to the English liberal rabbi responsible for
the liturgy: "Warm and affectionate regards to your
wife and children, and to all mankind."

Liebman concludes, "The Jew wished to be accepted
as an equal in society *not* because he was a Jew, but
because his Jewishness was *irrelevant.* Yet at the same
time, the Jew refused to make his own Jewishness
irrelevant. . . . He made . . . contradictory demands
on society. He wants to be accepted into the tradition
of society without adapting to the society's dominant
tradition." Minorities feel themselves "particular,"
view their traditions as "ritual," and distinguish between the private, unique, and personal, and the public,
universal, and commonplace. Majorities do not; they
accept the given. This constitutes the liberal dilemma:
how to affirm universalism and remain particular.

The "Jewish problem" is most commonly phrased
by young Jews as: Why should I be Jewish? I believe
in universal ideals — who needs particular ones as well?

Jews who ask the question "Why be Jewish?" testify
that "being Jewish" separates a person from the things
he or she wants. People who are different from the
majority frequently affirm that difference, but the affirmation may contain such excessive protest that it is
not much different from denial. The quintessential
datum of Jewish existence is anti-Semitism, along
with uncertainty of status, denial of normality, and
self-doubt.

Kurt Lewin pointed out that "every underprivileged

minority group is kept together not only by cohesive forces among its members but also by the boundary which the majority erects against the crossing of an individual from the minority to the majority" (*Resolving Social Conflicts: Selected Papers on Group Dynamics,* New York, 1948, p. 164). A member of an underprivileged group will try to gain in social status by joining the majority — to pass, to assimilate. The basic fact of life is this wish to cross the boundary, and hence, as Lewin says, the member of a minority group "lives almost perpetually in a state of conflict and tension. He dislikes . . . his own group because it is nothing but a burden to him. . . . A Jew of this type will dislike everything specifically Jewish, for he will see in it that which keeps him away from the majority for which he is longing." Such a Jew is the one who constantly asks, "Why be Jewish?" He is the one who fantasizes about a common religion of humanity and universal values that transcend, and incidentally obliterate, denominational and sectarian boundaries. It is no accident that the universal social movement (communism) and the universal psychology (Freudianism) were in large measure attractive to marginal Jews.

When Jews assimilate and try to blot out the marks of their particularity, they become another type of Jew — but they do not cease being Jewish. The real issue is never "to be or not to be a Jew" any more than the issue for me is to be or not to be my father's son. Lewin makes this wholly clear: "It is not similarity or dissimilarity of individuals that constitutes a group, but interdependence of fate." Jews brought up to think that being Jewish is chiefly, or only, a matter of religion soon discover that disbelieving in God does not make them non-Jews. They still are Jews; they still are obsessed by that fact and compelled to confront it, whether within the society of Jews or outside it.

Indeed, outside that society, Jewish consciousness becomes more intense. Among Jews one is a human being, with peculiarities and virtues of one's own. Among Gentiles one is a Jew, with traits common to the group one seeks to reject. That is probably why Jews still live in mostly Jewish neighborhoods and associate, outside business hours, mostly with other Jews. And when crisis comes, as it frequently does, then no one doubts that he shares a common cause, a common fate, with other Jews. Kurt Lewin says:

> In a minority group, individual members who are economically successful . . . usually gain a higher degree of acceptance by the majority group. This places them culturally on the periphery of the underprivileged group and makes them more likely to be "marginal" persons. . . . Nevertheless, they are frequently called for leadership by the underprivileged group because of their status and power. They themselves are usually eager to accept the leading role in the minority, partly as a substitute for gaining status in the majority. As a result, we find the rather paradoxical phenomenon. . . . Instead of having a group led by people who are proud of the group . . . we see minority leaders who are lukewarm toward the group.

This, I think, is true of United States Jewry.

As I said in the opening chapter, American Jews want to be Jewish, *but not too much so,* not so much that they cannot also be part of the imaginary undifferentiated majority. And herein lies their pathology. A human being does not begin as part of an undifferentiated mass. Once we leave the maternity ward, we go to a home of real people with a concrete history.

What does this mean for the community life of the Jews? Howard Singer has a name for the Jewish "Uncle Tom" — Cousin Merwyn (*Bring Forth the Mighty Men,* New York, 1969). Who is this Cousin Merwyn? He honors all religions — but his own. "He averts his eyes in embarrassment when he sees a Jew carrying a *lulav* on Sukkot, but he is touched and respectful when he sees Christians carrying palms on Palm Sunday." A Jewish bar mitzvah is loud and vulgar, but an Italian street festival is picturesque. But, Singer reports, there are two kinds of Merwyns. Merwyn Outside and Merwyn Inside. Merwyn Outside "will have nothing to do with anything Jewish. . . . Liberalism will have to serve as his kinship and his social milieu. . . . Merwyn Outside yearns to transcend his parochial origins." But Merwyn Inside is the more characteristic self-hating Jew.

> Merwyn Inside suffers from the same malady, but in another form. He, too, will flee his Jewishness, but his flight is disguised. His technique is to take the Jews with him, to make Jewish life less recognizably Jewish. He will join a synagogue, but suggest innovations in the religious service that will make it untraditional in spirit. When they are made he will not attend anyway. He will send his child to Sunday school, and perhaps join the religious school board, but he will oppose raising the educational standards on the grounds that the childrem are overburdened with Public School work. . . . With a sparkling conscience, and always in the name of "progress"

or good fellowship, he will vulgarize and corrode the institutions of Jewish life.

Merwyn Outside is merely a dead loss to the Jewish group, but Merwyn Inside is a galloping disaster. For Merwyn Inside is often wealthy, energetic, and willing to work. These qualities soon bring him into positions of influence and authority. And if American Jewish organizations have lost touch with Jewish needs, it is because Merwyn Inside dominates those organizations.

What then is to be done? In my view, nothing at all. Once one has explained a problem and persuaded people of its importance, he is supposed to announce the solution, found an organization, and ask people to write out checks. Everyone feels better. People have *done something.* But organizations administer no cure for self-hatred. It is part of the Jewish condition; it is the Jewish version of the human condition of self-devaluation.

Neverthless, rational perception itself is therapeutic: To know, to understand, to accept — these lead to healing and, in turn, to the transformation of neuroses into creative and redemptive forces. Let us recognize that ambivalence about being Jewish exists — with honesty, with compassion, and with dignity.

The Jewish Community
and the University Campus

Harvard asks for $15 million. Columbia asks for $7.5 million. And elsewhere, colleges and universities ask for millions more. Desperate for new sources of endowment, universities come to Jewish philanthropists and even to the organized Jewish community with proposals of grandiose programs, departments, professorships, of Jewish studies.

Let us savor the moment. Not too many years ago the universities would not take our money when we tried to give it to them for Jewish studies. Jewish money might be laundered — made more American — in a few particularly liberal places. But in general, universities didn't want our children, our money, or our culture, in approximately that rising order of disdain.

How are we to respond to the new situation? Should the organized Jewish community or Jewish philanthropists as individuals respond to current and future drives? If they should, then on what basis and for what purpose?

Let me start with a visit I paid to a small college in Pennsylvania about ten years ago. At that time I was asked to "help plan" a program in the study of Judaism within the Department of Religion. I quickly discovered that my "help" was supposed to consist of advising the college's "development officer" (fund-raiser) on how to approach Jewish donors and foundations. The college had in mind nothing short of an endowed professorship, which cost $500,000. My response to this plan was brief. If I were asked whether or not a philanthropist with money to spend for Jewish studies should endow a chair at Franklin and Marshall, my response would be: Whatever for? Who would take such a position *who also should have it?* Very few people of such distinction as to deserve endowed professorships were then (or are now) available. The field is young, and the people in it mainly beginning their time of creativity and productivity. We have yet to see important achievements in the field as a whole. More important, if an endowed chair is to be created, why should it be at that particular college? What achievements in the study of Judaism can this college put forward as evidence that a major, endowed chair should now come forth in response to demonstrated competence and even excellence?

This is what I would advise the Jewish community and Jewish philanthropists to ask those who come with vast and inflated claims on Jewish support. It is reasonable to ask why we should invest money in a company, with its particular management, record of earnings, and prospects. So too with universities: Why you? Why now? What for? And the answers must include attention to solid achievement.

Achievement comes in several distinct forms. First is educational achievement. Does your university now have a program in some aspect of the diverse fields of Jewish studies? If not, why not start one and show us what you can do *before* you ask us to bear the burden of its future? If you do have a program, tell me about its courses and, of greater importance, the shape of its curriculum. What educational goal stands behind the diverse courses you now offer? What does a student learn who completes your program of studies? What place does this learning have in the student's growth to maturity in thinking and understanding?

Second is scholarly achievement. Professors have the time to increase their knowledge and to contribute to what we know about their subjects. If they teach two or three courses a term, as most do, then they have a sizable block of time reserved for reading, thinking, reflecting, and writing. How do they use this time? Is your university a center for scholarly achievement? In what ways has your faculty contributed in the past to the knowledge of Judaism, or the understanding of Jewish history, literature, or society today? Granted, scholarly expression takes many forms. But surely there are significant ways to contribute to learning, if not in books, then in articles, if not in writing, then in important lectures at learned society meetings or at other universities, and above all, in the minds of students.

Third is contribution to the academic community at large. Endowments are meant to make a lasting impact upon the formation of a field and upon the shape of learning in the academic community outside one's own university and in other fields within one's own university — a tall order, but millions of dollars for endowment are also a tall order. In what ways has your program in Jewish learning had its impact (even if in negative ways, through experiments that have not worked) upon the formation of the larger field of Jewish learning? What influence have you had, whether positive or negative, upon the definition of the subject, the way it is taught, and the manner in which scholarly projects are worked out?

The most impressive items in the universities' vast demands for Jewish money are the grandiose claims and the inflated self-praise in the printed literature. But one looks in vain for concrete facts to support these claims, facts about today, not about what a now retired or deceased professor accomplished, with little support or recognition from the university that now invokes his name.

Columbia University wants $7.5 million, but Columbia has yet to wield the influence and force it demonstrated in Salo Baron's age, down to the early 1960s. In Jewish learning it is as isolationist and self-absorbed as Harvard.

The search by Harvard University for $15 million relies in its fund-raising literature mainly upon the achievements of Harry Wolfson. But its brochures prove remarkably reticent about its present resources in Judaic studies, as pursued by Jewish professors of Jewish studies. Non-Jewish professors of Jewish studies are bypassed in silence, as if they were not at Harvard at all!

No one would take seriously a stock issue whose

prospectus excluded all reference to current problems awaiting attention and solution. But there is no Securities and Exchange Commission to supervise the business of learning, nor does a Pure Food and Drug Act, or a Truth in Advertising Act, govern the solicitations of universities.

The organized Jewish community has not fully worked out a policy and a program for universities and for Jewish scholarship. The National Foundation for Jewish Culture, created in part to deal with the academic agenda, has foundered, never receiving much support, rarely deserving more support than it received. Meanwhile a sizable list of problems awaits attention, and money will not solve them until a policy exists to deal with them. Still, there are a few areas in which modest sums will do no harm.

It is time for the Jewish community to consider how it will support those young men and women who wish to devote their lives to the academic pursuit of Jewish learning in its diverse disciplines. Right now, there is no communal source for fellowships in Jewish learning. Once people reach the dissertation stage, they are able to turn to the National Foundation for Jewish Culture. But before that time, they must struggle alone to support themselves and secure opportunities to study abroad and at one or more universities at home, as is often needed.

It is time for the Jewish community to ask how the results of scholarly work are to be disseminated. These books and journals rarely are able to pay their own way, since, in the nature of things, the audience is small. Now that library budgets for acquisitions are less ample, even purchases in academic collections tend to be limited. As a result manuscripts, including carefully constructed dissertations and important monographs by mature scholars, do not easily find their way into print. Remarkably small sums can both solve this problem and provide for copies of scholarly books to be placed in Jewish community libraries. Yet the funds are not available.

It is time for the Jewish community to decide whether or not it has a stake in ongoing scholarly research. I simply do not believe that the leadership of the organized community is indifferent to anything that is not practical or that has no Israeli angle. But that is how matters now appear. The great anthropologist Adolf E. Jensen remarks, "The spiritual creations of Western culture — religions, great works of art, the *Geisteswissenschaften,* for example — know of no such practical purposes." Is it possible that those same Jews who form the cadres of leadership in institutions of music, art, drama, and literature in North America are wholly closed to the requirements of Jewish culture, including its scholarly component? Are we proud that the National Endowment for the Humanities and the National Endowment for the Arts currently invest vast sums in Jewish scholarship and culture, while the Jewish communities starve the institutions of Jewish learning — seminaries, colleges of education, and the like — and treat with callous indifference the achievements of Jewish learning?

It is one thing to ask for signs of solid achievement.

It is another to neglect those solid achievements already in hand. I think that, as proud and self-respecting people, we have every right to expect universities to justify their Gargantuan appetites for Jewish money and Jewish learning. But as proud and self-respecting people we must also follow the example of the federal government and take seriously those intangible treasures of the spirit even now languishing in our midst.

We need a cogent and thoughtful policy to help the organized community and individual philanthropists form opinions and make decisions on the needs of the hour and on the proper demands, laid before us even now, on behalf of the future. Since all of us believe that there is a viable and interesting future for Jews in North America, we have also to lay foundations for a viable and interesting intellectual and cultural life for those coming generations.

Orthodoxy:
(1) Arrogance and Authenticity

When you consider the power of Judaism, realized most fully and profoundly in Orthodoxy, you must wonder why every Jew should not be Orthodox and Judaic — not merely Jewish. The grandeur of the Judaic perspective on humanity, the extraordinary relevance of that perspective to everyday practice, the ineffable beauty of the consequent way of living, a holy way of living, separate and distinct, in full measure congruent with the profound meaning of our mortality and our human striving — what is life without that vision? And how can people turn their backs on it?

Who are we when we do not live up to that image which is God's and ours? And what can we be when we fully reckon with that image? This, to me, is what shapes the transcendent and compelling call to Orthodoxy, the true Judaic way of life.

And yet. And yet, the great majority of North American Jews who choose to be religious also choose not to be Orthodox, and a near majority of them choose not to be religious at all. So there is the paradox: the power and mystery of Judaism on the one hand, the indifference of the Jews to Judaism on the other. Since, we must all agree, Orthodoxy is the fullest expression of Judaism, we surely have the right to turn to Orthodoxy for some insight into the current paradox.

Nor should we underestimate the force of that paradox. When young Jews wish to resume the holy way given up by their parents or grandparents — when they become *baalei teshuvah,* "reverters" to Judaism — what is it to which they revert? It is the Orthodox way. That fact accounts for the growing traditionalism of the Judaism in the Jewish Theological Seminary and Conservative branch, and even for the kosher eating facilities at Hebrew Union College.

People perceive, and I think rightly, that Orthodoxy keeps the Grail (to use an inappropriate but weighty metaphor) of the holy way of life called Judaism. So when they return, they take for granted that it must be to Orthodoxy. And many others will concur that Orthodoxy is the standard by which all Judaism is measured.

And so it is — alas!

For if we claim that the keepers of the Grail have allowed it to become tarnished, who can disagree? Surely that grand perspective of who we are and what we may become, of ourselves in God's likeness and in accord with God's image, is lost. Are we not told by students of every cult and crackpot outfit, from Jews for Jesus to Reverend Moon, that Jews make up, not 3 or 4 percent of their followers, but 16 to 60 percent? (Moon tells us the Jews must be a very holy people, because they produce so many members for his church.) And sociologists tell us again and again that the young Jews (among others) in these cults go there for something they do not find at home, for a vivid life of the soul, a seeking after God and holiness that they cannot perceive in Judaism!

Still, why draw evidence from marginal people ("apostates")? And why indict the keepers of the Grail for conditions so far beyond their control? There is better proof, nearer to the center of things, that greatness is gone from Orthodoxy and therefore from Judaism: There is evidence not only of omission — to which, after all, Orthodoxy can plausibly plead extenuating circumstances. There is evidence of commission as well. When an Orthodox Jew says, "He is very religious," what follows? Does he say that "he is a person who fears God" or "who loves his fellow man"? No. More likely, "He waits seven hours between milk and meat." Or, "He eats only *glatt kosher*." Or, "He won't even eat a hard-boiled egg in the home of a Conservative rabbi."

Everyone knows this measure of religiosity, and it is always by a standard of religious practice of ritualistic character. It is as if Orthodoxy wishes to glorify every item of ritualism and self-righteousness that the enemies of Judaism have used to challenge Judaism over four centuries, since Luther.

It would be unfair to invoke, in this context, the names of Orthodox rabbis who were tried and convicted of exploitation of old and sick people. Nor are we interested in the many examples of a certain Orthodox indifference to ethics when "outsiders" are concerned. These are not the issues. The issue is how we may describe the face of Orthodoxy to the Jewish world itself, to Reform and Conservative Jews, and to the "nonreligious."

Does Orthodoxy approach that world with love and affection? Is its message one of the sanctification of all Israel, of the precious worth and holy meaning of every Jewish soul? Does Orthodoxy rejoice in the (admittedly imperfect) efforts of the non-Orthodox religious Jew to keep the faith and practice it?

Challenged with its greatest opportunity in nearly two hundred years to regain the attention of the Jewish people, confronted by a generation of reversion to Judaism, the face of Orthodoxy is frowning, not smiling. Its message is a tale of contempt to the non-Orthodox religious Jews. Except for the handful able to adopt the Orthodox way of life in all details and assimilate into Orthodox circles, Orthodoxy has only ugly and unfriendly words. Orthodoxy does not love the Jewish people — unless they are Orthodox.

It did not have to be this way. There were great Orthodox rabbis who came to westernized Jews with messages of love, with hope for a return (which finally has come about, but not under Orthodox auspices in the main). Israel Salanter in the nineteenth century, the great Palestinian chief rabbi, Rav Kook, in the twentieth — these are only two names revered by all Jews. When Jewry was unready, Orthodoxy sent forth leaders of good sense and good will. Now that the Jews are ready, ready to hear the authentic message of holiness and the Torah as spoken by Orthodox voices, Orthodoxy — with only a few exceptions — speaks gibberish, and with a grimace to boot.

What, after all, is the human message of Orthodoxy? Out of the chosenness of Israel and the holiness of the Land of Israel, Orthodoxy in the State of Israel (with powerful support from North America) has made an irredentist and militarist, pseudo-Messianic ideal of keeping everything we can and throwing out the rest. True, there was Joshua. But there was also Isaiah.

Out of the holy way of life, a mode of living meant to sanctify each gesture and each moment, a way of life supposed to open our hearts to God and our minds to the Torah, Orthodoxy has created a pattern of trivia and nonsense, a set of humanly irrelevant gestures, practiced in a spirit of punctilious pride. Would that this judgment were wrong. It does not go far enough.

A simple example will suffice. More emotional energy is invested in whether or not a given kosher butcher shop is sufficiently kosher than in whether or not the everyday speech of the customers is kosher. What goes into the mouth hardly matters so much as what comes out of the mouth, but Orthodox rabbis rarely tell us about that fundamental teaching of Judaism. Attitudes toward non-Orthodox Jews, or Orthodox Jews unlike those in one's own circle, range from loveless to hateful. In America and even more so in Israel, Orthodoxy presents the larger Jewish community with an angry, scowling face. The principle of *ahavat Yisrael* "love for Israel," the Jewish people, has lost all hold on Orthodox Judaism, which, in that aspect, must be regarded as a Judaic heresy.

Out of the Holy Torah, an intellectual tradition of amazing brilliance and continuing power, Orthodoxy has fashioned a set of propositions of dubious truth and little fact. The next chapter spells this out in detail. A once reasonable tradition of religious learning now requires the denial of facts in the name of faith. It is only an accident that some *rav* has not yet declared a fundamental article of faith to be belief that the world is flat. Yeshivas, for their part, treat learning as pure ritual, so that merely repeating words, without understanding what they mean, is taken as a holy act.

And when we turn to the "modern Orthodox" and ask them for a Jewish message, what do we hear? We hear politics, polemics, and right-wing slogans (especially where the State of Israel is concerned), smug diatribes against Conservative and Reform Judaism. Parades of words, spoken without passion and conceived without anguish, words that say absolutely nothing — and do so insultingly.

In a different context, Ray Sokolov recently evaluated Robert Gordis's new book on Judaism and sex: "The real problem with this book is that it cannot hope to persuade thousands of apostate Jews of anything except that they were right to abandon formal Jewish observance — not so much because of the rigid views of the rabbinate, but because of the irrelevant and empty language that 'modern' leaders . . . spew out in a simplistic and vacant attempt to win young people back to the fold. . . . Such rhetoric says nothing and makes the skeptic yawn. Such mindless sermonizing is exactly what has driven many modern Jews into secular forms of Jewish life."

The critique is even more appropriate when applied

to the Orthodox. It is simply not the case, as "outsiders" sometimes imagine, that Orthodoxy — unlike the Reform and Conservative movements — speaks clearly and decisively. The difference is that it hides its confusion behind a mask of authenticity. It is Orthodoxy that claims — and I think fairly and rightly — to be authentic and (in its vulgar and embarrassing phrase) "Torah-true." But precisely because its claim is fair and right, its expression of that claim is tragic, its arrogant demeanor an offense. Valid authenticity is no substitute for thought or for manners. It does not excuse either self-righteousness or the affectation of certainty.

For beyond and above Orthodoxy, organized and unorganized, lies the Judaism that is still best preserved in its richness and its mystery by Orthodoxy itself. We cannot forget, after all, that the Torah studied by Orthodoxy and in mindless yeshivas is still the Hebrew Bible and the Talmud. The Pentateuch and the Prophets are read fully and accurately in Orthodox synagogues. The works of the great rationalists, like Maimonides, the great mystics, like the Besht, still are opened and taken seriously — for more than a fifty-minute classroom lecture — by the Orthodox. When Jews wants to live by the teachings of the great souls and minds of a tradition of four thousand years, they rightly turn to Orthodoxy. And that is precisely why we have a right to ask of Orthodoxy, for its part, that it take seriously the methods and meanings of those teachings. Let us now turn to a specific case.

Orthodoxy:
(2) *Lernen* and Learning

Since contemporary Orthodox Judaism both in North
America and in the State of Israel regards itself as the
sole "legitimate" and "authentic" form of Judaism
and all others are heretical, we have to ask whether the
practice of Orthodoxy validates that claim. When we
compare the way Orthodox Jews *actually* carry out
long-established and classical rites of the Judaism we
know from the canonical documents with what the
authoritative texts of Judaism in its formative age say
about those rites, what do we see? For the claim that
"we alone are authentic" surely demands testing
against the criterion of authenticity supplied by the
very books that the Orthodox, along with all other religious Jews, regard as the Torah, that is, books that
contain God's will for Israel, the Jewish people.

Now one principal mode of expressing piety in Judaism, classical and contemporary alike, consists in the
simple act of learning the holy books. It is the act of
"study of the Torah," or studying in a group of pious
Jews and with an authoritative teacher, a rabbi, a written passage of the Torah. If you join a group of Jews
who are sitting together and reading and discussing a
book of the Hebrew Bible along with the readings of

classical exegetes, or a passage of the Talmud (or an equivalent document from the canon of Judaism), you then perform the religious act of "study of the Torah."

That "study of the Torah," moreover, takes place in every setting in which Orthodox Judaism flourishes. It constitutes the critical, the key, the authentic, the religious act, the very essence of piety. So we have every right to ask whether and how studying the Torah, or *lernen,* as it is carried on today in Orthodox Judaism in North America compares to the way in which Torah study is represented in the classical documents of Judaism, the Hebrew Bible as interpreted by the Talmud, for example.

In what follows, I focus upon a recent and authoritative account of how the Torah is studied as an avocation by Jews who, in doing so, deem themselves to be pious. I draw the contrast between the substance of the symbol — Torah learning — and the manner in which the symbol reaches social reality, that is, Torah study by amateurs in synagogue and yeshiva alike. The symbol over the centuries had gained weighty and dense intellectual substance. Today the same symbol turns out to be invoked to stand for an activity of slight intellectual substance. Study of the Torah turns out to constitute a ritual of little study and virtually no torah. What that fact about the contemporary status of the ancient symbol suggests beyond itself I cannot say. We already know that symbol change is social change, and that the Jews exhibit symptons of fundamental social change.

Everybody knows that the Jews are the people of the

Book, as Mohammed called them, but also the people whose religious life centers around the study of holy books. It is a commonplace that through the work of studying those books, people express their piety and seek to attain holiness. Now that cannot be regarded as "pretty much how things are," for, we know, in other religious traditions piety comes about in other ways, for example, through a life of poverty and service to the poor, or through heroism on the battlefield in the service of the faith, or through holy vagrancy, celibacy, saying prayers, and so on through a long list. It is distinctive to Judaism that when you study certain books, you are changed, made holy.

The word in Yiddish is *lernen,* and it means a spiritual meditation on Jewish books of a certain character. Some "learned" full time, and many did some of the time. The important fact is that we deal, in *lernen,* or in Talmud Torah, with something more than the mere acquisition of facts. People misconstrue the issue if they think that when Jews express piety through the study of the Torah, they come only or mainly for information.

In a brilliant work of ethnography, *The People of the Book: Drama, Fellowship, and Religion* (Chicago, 1983), Samuel Heilman tells how he set out to write a book about Jews who study the Torah, or "learn," as an avocation. (He does not treat those who do it all the time.) He noticed the fact to which I just now alluded, namely, at issue was not merely the acquisition of knowledge, but something else. In that connection he makes an important observation.

From early on I realized that, for many of the Jews I was observing, this experience was more than simply the assimilation of knowledge. For one thing, many of those I watched had been *lernen* for years, but still seemed to be unable to review the texts on their own or recall very much of the content in front of them. For another, even those who had *lernt* a lot and displayed an erudite familiarity with the texts took apparent great pleasure in repeating what they had already studied rather than looking for the new and as yet unknown. The best *lernen,* it seemed, was the sort which reiterated what everyone already knew. The best questions to ask were those the texts themselves asked; and the best if not the only true answers were those already written on the pages open before one. Finally, while the members of the study circles I observed ostensibly gathered in the house of study to get the wisdom of Judaism from the books into their minds, they often spent more time in class getting their feelings about Judaism off their chests. *Clearly much more than learning or the accumulation of information about Jewish texts was going on. I wanted to find out what that something more was* (italics supplied; Heilman, p. 2).

Heilman's reflections on what he saw in many years of observing the process of study of the Torah, or *lernen,* present us with a puzzle. We take for granted that we learn in order to know a particular subject; we know in order to understand a particular subject. Learning is a process of problem solving. It helps us to understand, to appreciate. When we learn, we grow, we change, we live our lives in a framework of greater comprehension, in a larger dimension of meaning.

That description of what I believe people do when they learn omits reference to the one dimension important in Talmud Torah or *lernen.* When we study arithmetic, or even ethics, we do not claim to become holy men and women. We become better informed; we may even improve our intellectual powers; we might even turn out to be happier or possibly better human beings. But the dimension of holiness measures nothing, defines nothing, affects nothing. And for the processes of Talmud Torah or *lernen,* the ultimate goal is sanctification. What is learned may appear to be secular facts. But the source of what is learned, which is Torah, and the intent of the ones who do the learning, which is to study the Torah, reshape the intellectual act into a religious quest, a holy event.

When Heilman states that among hobbyists he observed "more than simply the assimilation of knowledge," he points toward what distinguishes the act of study of the Torah from all other acts of learning, the setting of the study house and circle of rabbi and disciples from all other situations of intellect, and the process of teaching and studying the Torah from all other processes by which people enlarge their intellects and enhance their knowledge. And yet, the act remains the same: the use of the mind, the formation of a social group for the acquisition of knowledge, and — it is always a social group — the improvement of one's status. How different is this act of learning, which is different from all other acts of learning, this Talmud Torah, this realm of *lernen?* The verbal explanation invokes language and images not routinely associated with schooling and study. But the act itself — use of the mind — remains what it is. Whether you use your power of understanding to study history or Jewish law, to master mathematics or the traditional interpretation of the Hebrew Scriptures, the power that you use remains what it is.

If that is the case, then we must find astonishing Heilman's characterization of this "experience" that is "more than simply the assimilation of knowledge." Heilman makes three points. First, the students after many years do not learn very much: "unable to review the texts on their own or recall very much of the content in front of them." My own observations of students who return to my university — and they were not hobbyists — after a year of study in an Israeli yeshiva correspond to Heilman's. When I ask them what they learned, they name the tractate. When I ask them the main point of the tractate, or of the part of it they supposedly learned, they are dumfounded. They never learned. Unlike university learning, their process of study involved reading little or nothing on their own, writing nothing on their own, pursuing no questions beyond those raised and answered in the classroom. And the class in Torah study, as I am able to investigate its properties, consists of a river of words, flowing out of the mouth of the rabbi, scarcely eddying up to the shores, into the overstuffed ears of the disciple. Learning that does not equip the students to do on their own what the teacher teaches yields, not education, but "something else."

Heilman observed, second, that the students enjoy repeating what they know. The process is one of rehearsing the message, saying in intricately subtle ways what everyone knows, reaffirming the given. Learning thus forms a labor, not of discovery and testing, but of repetition and revalidation. Then the relationship of teacher to student finds definition in the authority of the one, the subordination of the other, the affirmation of the teacher's authority by the student, the reassurance of the student by the teacher. Learning becomes a process not of discovery but of renewal, not of inquiry and the testing of possibilities but of displaying, in intellectual form, one's loyalty and devotion to the revealed truths of the faith. So, as Heilman says, the students took "great pleasure in repeating what they had already studied rather than looking for the new and as yet unknown. The best *lernen* . . . was the sort which reiterated what everyone already knew." You ask only when you know the answer, and the purpose of asking is to hear the reassuring and familiar answer.

Finally, Heilman pointed out that a great deal of class time is spent in free-associating, expressing how people feel, chatting about this and that — all under the auspices of God and revealed Torah. Heilman says that among the hobbyists whom he studied, "much more than learning . . . was going on." But his book demonstrates that a great deal *less* than learning also was going on: experience, not intellect; emotion, not disciplined speculation and imagination; transactions of a private and individual character, not a public exchange of reasoned and well-constructed argument. If people come to class to get "their feelings about Judaism off their chests," then they do not come to learn at all. For the one thing you do not do when you tell people how you feel is learn something about the world beyond yourself.

Heilman may have to face the charge of misinterpreting what he saw. But I doubt anyone can make the charge stick. For he details what he observed over many years, in many settings of avocational *lernen,* and, in my more limited experience, the anecdotes he reports, the generalizations he draws, the picture he composes, do indeed capture the reality of *lernen* or Talmud Torah in our day. Perhaps in some remote or isolated place a quite different transaction takes place when people as a hobby or avocation open the holy books of Judaism with the same intent that brings them to do so in yeshivas and related settings, namely, to attain sanctification. But in the main, *lernen* is ritual learning. And ritual learning has nothing to do with the two things we in the secular West associate with the intellect: learning and attaining understanding.

To state matters simply, *lernen* and learning have little to do with one another. We teachers aim through teaching to make ourselves obsolete. We want our students to be able to do things on their own. If my students after many years could not review texts on their own or remember the content before them, I should regard my teaching as worthless. If my students could only repeat what I say, without critical examination and renewal, I should regard my teaching as hopeless. If my classroom were a place in which people mainly free-associated about whatever they had on their minds, a place with no program and no purpose, I should regard my teaching as pointless. So far as Heilman's characterization of the something more — and the something less — of Talmud Torah or *lernen* as he saw it proves accurate, therefore, I have to judge the so-called traditional setting for Jewish learning as worthless, hopeless, and pointless.

Does Jewish learning in a secular context exhibit worth, hope, a point? What difference does it make if, as in the academy, the labor points not toward the sanctification of the student, the rehearsal of the preaching of the faith, the validation and reaffirmation of "the tradition," but toward discovery and renewal of interest and insight? To these questions we have now to turn. For the task of public discourse of intellect is not to celebrate but to analyze. Were I merely to propose a new intellectual orthodoxy to take the place of a discredited and decayed old one, I should serve no lasting end. Indeed, it is not my purpose merely to add to the injuries already inflicted upon the tradition of Jewish learning by the practitioners of *lernen*. What I wish to propose is that *lernen* as Heilman describes it bears no true witness to *lernen* as the great masters of Talmud Torah have practiced it in the past and, in some few instances, vocational students practice it today as well.

Let me then present two propositions. First, the one just now introduced: *Lernen* as Heilman portrays it and Talmud Torah as the classic texts of Judaism portray it bear slight resemblance to one another. Second, the sources for the renewal of a truly intellectual encounter with Jewish tradition flow from those same attitudes of mind that we today cultivate in the secular academy: criticism, freedom of imagination and inquiry, devotion to learning as a process of enlightment, a quest for understanding.

Anyone who opens the classical texts of Judaism, from the Mishnah onward through the two Talmuds, the various compositions organized around the exegesis of Scripture, the speculative works of philosophers and mystics, the constructive works of legal codifiers and social philosophers of Judaism, onward through the remarkably original creations of modern times in Hasidism, in Hebrew literature, in modern Jewish thought and learning — anyone familiar with even a book, even a chapter, even a sentence, of that vast corpus must assent to one claim. When we study the Torah, we are meant to encounter matters of intellect, ideas, problems of inquiry. Study of the Torah begins (though it does not and should not end) with the use of our minds. When, moreover, we do use our mind, *it is to learn.* No authentic master of the Torah in its thirty-five hundred years of unfolding can agree that study of the Torah characterizes the accomplishment of people who cannot review on their own or remember much of what they are supposed to have learned. Ritual learning has nothing to do with study of the Torah, even though, in sizable circles, studying the Torah constitutes little more than an empty ritual.

Study of the Torah assuredly requires us to repeat and even to memorize. There is no learning without acquisition of facts, of texts and their contents, accurately interpreted. The opposite of learning is making

things up as we go along. That we cannot do if we wish
to stand within the rigorous tradition of Talmud Torah.
But when you study the Talmud, you reason. When
you take up the commentaries to the written Torah,
you must try to understand the questions they ask, the
answers they offer. Learning requires more than rehearsing the message, repeating what we hear like
dumbbells. Learning means understanding, and understanding transcends mere repetition of what others
have explained, repeating holy words like incantations.
True, not everyone can attain a high level of reasoning,
of critical inquiry. But few are so ungifted that they
cannot do more than repeat, without true comprehension, two and two are four, or "In the beginning God
created the world," or "When do people recite the
Shema in the evening?" The notion that when we learn
we mainly define a relationship to an authority figure,
moreover, contradicts the purpose of learning defined
in every text of Judaism. That purpose is simple. We
learn in order to carry out what we learn, not merely
to replicate the teacher. It goes without saying that in
order to do something intelligently and sincerely, we
must not only assent to but also understand the truth
at hand. Anything else means merely to go through the
motions. Talmud Torah is meant to create greater,
more holy human beings, not oxen and dumb asses.

All of the texts of Judaism, early and late, exhibit
the single trait of careful organization, deeply reflective purpose. Talmud Torah brings us to texts that
always make a point, always follow a program, always
seek to impact meaning. True, that meaning, the order

and purpose, may not always rise to the surface. But no text of Judaism is mere gibberish. None involves only free association. The two Talmuds sometimes are misrepresented as formless and aimless, a mere mass of this-and-that. But people who so represent the Talmuds have not carefully inquired into the reasons that their materials follow the order that they do, rather than some other order or no order at all. Everyone who has covered the whole of a tractate can explain the order of that tractate. Anyone familiar with more than a few lines, chosen haphazardly, recognizes that principles of form and logic govern the layout of the literature. So when people think that Talmud Torah permits or even requires free association, they misconstrue the substance and the form, the aesthetics and the logic, of the Torah. True enough, Talmud Torah speaks to our hearts and not only to our minds. When we study the Torah we gain not only information but also experience. We feel as well as think, experience emotion as well as gain insight. But all of this rightly done responds to the plan and the order of our texts: We feel the emotions the founders and dreamers of our texts wanted us to feel, our hearts respond to the heartfelt plea of the words carefully chosen by the authors in order to engage us. Indeed, when we study the Torah without committing the heart, the imagination, the emotion, we gain mere information, and little enough of that.

The right route to the heart of the Torah leads outward *from* the Torah. Our learning requires us to bring the teachings of the Torah to our context. We carry

the text outward to the context. In the avocational
lernen Heilman describes, the context defines the text, what people bring to the text dictates what the text will be permitted to say. That is why Heilman finds so much free association, so little attention to the issue at hand. The issue at hand is the Torah, and the task is to study the Torah. That by definition constitutes the program of the classroom, the curriculum, the teacher's plan. If *lernen* happens when people come to class to get "their feelings about Judaism off their chests," as Heilman says, then *lernen* has nothing to do with the Torah. It is something we make up as we go along.

Let me summarize this part of the argument. *Lernen* as Heilman portrays it and Talmud Torah as the classic texts of Judaism portray it bear slight resemblance to one another. That negative argument sets the stage for the positive proposition I wish to offer. It is, as I said, that those same attitudes that define our work in the secular academy also dictate how we should do our work in the sacred circle of Talmud Torah.

What we seek in our classrooms is for students not only to learn but also to learn *how.* It is not enough to master the facts. We want our students to know how people think, the methods, not only the results, of learning.

We seek, further, not merely to repeat knowledge but to renew learning. What this means is to rediscover the logic, the principles of order and structure, that dictate knowledge. For that purpose merely repeating what we know is never enough. Every good course promises to look for the new, leads students into the unknown. History 2 does not go over the immutable truths of History 1.

Finally, in our classrooms we come with a purpose in mind, and we do our best to carry out that purpose. The teacher's work requires more than the mere validation of the students' value. There is a prior, overriding program of learning. The conception that when we come together, it is to tell one another how we feel contradicts everything for which we stand. For the mind does its work only when it follows logic and discovers order.

Now when you turn to the texts that we study when we study the Torah, what traits of mind do we discern? First, in the Talmuds we find stress on the flow of argument, on the use of the critical intellect, on the promise of disagreement and critical discussion. Indeed, the two Talmuds and most of the writings that flow from them deal more with the "how" of learning than with the "what." The facts change from tractate to tractate. The methods of critical reasoning remain always uniform, everywhere operative and applicable. So, as I said, Talmud Torah demands more than merely erudite repetition of what everyone knows.

Second, the substance of Talmud Torah spreads out over an enormous number of books, a vast area of learning. By definition, standing still, repeating some one thing, will not do. The new and the unknown lie always before; no one masters the whole. Everyone undertakes an unending voyage through the worlds of the Torah. The very character of the Torah dictates

the purpose of Talmud Torah, and given the breadth
and diversity of the Torah, no one can find satisfaction
in repeating a few simple sayings.

And I hardly need to restate the simple fact that
free association and Talmud Torah are enemies of one
another.

Since I find it self-evident that the character of the
Torah and the traits of *lernen* bear nothing in common, I must ask why so vast a world today assumes
that the true, the "authentic" mode of Judaic studies,
of study of Torah, of *lernen,* emerges from the circles,
in synagogues and in yeshivas, described by Heilman.
How can people who claim to be the *only* ones who
know "the Torah" and who insist they are the *only*
ones with sufficient erudition to say what "the Torah"
says also exhibit so little interest in the substance and
the form of Talmud Torah as these emerge from the
books of the Torah themselves? My best guess is that
the emperor is simply naked. The great traditions of
learning embodied in classical yeshivas, and embodied
even in our own day in some yeshivas, have lost their
hold on the bulk of Orthodoxy, as well as on those
Conservative and Reform rabbis who use the same
language and claim to teach the same texts in the same
way. Heilman describes not so much yeshivas as circles
of students formed by lay people in association with
rabbis who once studied in yeshivas. He will find in
Conservative and Reform synagogues analogous
groups.

So far as Talmud Torah has been turned by the
rabbinate into ritual learning, the fault lies not with

the great yeshivas but with their inferior products. So far as rivers of unfelt words drown in free association all sense, order, and meaning in the sacred texts, the reason is that those who spew out the stream of words do not know how to speak sensibly and pointedly. In yeshivas and equivalent seminaries they did not learn. But that does not necessarily mean they were not taught. So far as people hold on to the known, which they repeat and cherish, it is because they know only a little, and have not got much to tell other people. So far as the teacher tolerates free association, it is because then his authority remains secure, despite his limited learning. The main thing is for everyone to feel good and be happy, feel holy and be reassured. For that purpose, learning scarcely matters; *lernen* is not about learning anyhow. So, in a word, *lernen* as Heilman describes it testifies to the inauthenticity of its practitioners. It tells us that the very thing they claim to know they do not really understand at all.

Yet, may we in the academy, who study and teach Judaic texts, claim superiority over those who practice *lernen* in yeshivas, seminaries, synagogues, and temples?

So far as professors of Judaic studies engage in ethnic celebration and see their task as repeating and reaffirming the *kerygma* of whatever Judaism they espouse, they too carry out ritual learning.

So far as professors of Judaic studies lay claim to special standing and engage in special pleading, treat the Jews as essentially different from other groups, and analyze the Jews and Judaism through canons of in-

quiry and reason inapplicable elsewhere, they too practice *lernen,* not learning.

To the measure that the academic sector of Jewish
learning defines its work as the reading of prescribed
texts, with slight interest in the *how* but obsession
only with the *what,* the academic sector is not better
than the religious one. Indeed, it is worse, since the
practitioners of *lernen* at least do not claim to do something different from what has traditionally been done,
while the professors of Judaic studies celebrate the
difference.

Above all, to that degree that academic studies of
the Jews and Judaism prove repetitive and unproduc-
tive, creative only of boredom, incapable of asking new
questions and answering them in fresh ways, to that
degree the allegedly secular goes over the ground of
the supposedly religious and traditional teacher. In my
view the state of Judaic studies in the academy scarcely
improves upon the level of *lernen* in yeshivas and synagogues, except in its remarkable pretense at secularity,
sustained in a setting of nearly unrelieved ritualism.

To return to the main point, ritual learning is not
learning, and the notion that we "study Torah" when
we sit around and shoot the breeze is contemptible.
Torah study demanded, and still demands, intellectual
rigor and care. True, not everyone will master everything, and each person will achieve matters at his or
her own level. But there is a difference between lazi-
ness and self-indulgence on the one side and intellectual
limitations on the other. We cannot do it all, but in

not trying but pretending we "study Torah," we do nothing at all. In this, as in other ways, contemporary Jews turn out to err when they turn to Orthodoxy as the model for authentic Judaism. Authenticity lies with the Torah, not with people who claim, on the basis of so little solid achievement and so much pretension, alone and to the exclusion of all other Jews, to speak in behalf of the Torah.

The Rabbinate:
Torah and Learning

Every profession has its thinkers and its doers, just as, in the case of Judaism, we have professors of Judaic studies and rabbis. In medicine hospitals bridge the gap between medical research and practice, with seminars on current developments important for practicing physicians. In law the doers keep up with the thinkers because they have to; it is an adversary profession, so people have to keep learning. After nearly twenty-five years of teaching in universities I have to observe that, in general, we have yet to bridge the gap between the scholars of Judaic studies in universities and the pulpit rabbinate.

To state matters simply, with rare exceptions, the pulpit rabbis pay no attention at all to the scholarly and educational work in Judaic studies in universities. Important books are published, but rabbis do not read them. New ideas emerge, in literary, historical, and religious studies of Judaism, of which rabbis seldom take advantage.

Indeed, apart from a slight interest in biblical studies and contemporary Jewish politics, rabbis tend to ignore that vast middle range of Jewish experience represented by the entire corpus of rabbinical literature and Jewish philosophy from the Second to the Third Jewish Commonwealths. A kind of neo-Karaism comes out of the pulpit, which treats the rabbinical sources as a mere corpus of proof texts to be used however one wants to make a point one has thought up that morning. Thus we hear from the pulpit echoes of ideas conceived in another age, and we scarcely hear resonance of a full and rich encounter with that rabbinical canon, reopened in our own time, that marks us as distinctively Judaic: heirs of Moses' one whole Torah.

More important still, on the campus over the past quarter century a revolution in "Jewish education" — the transmission of learning in Judaism — has taken place. Thousands of young Jews have passed through courses in Judaic studies in universities all over the country. They have read books, heard lectures, participated in rigorous discussion, undertaken studies in the State of Israel. From the pulpit we hear messages aimed at Jews who have not read books and participated in informed and critical discussions, who have not learned how to listen to lectures in a sustained and careful way. The congregants in numbers become sophisticated in a reading of Judaic tradition that the rabbinate wishes to pretend has not taken place.

So a dream has come true, and the rabbis in general pretend nothing has happened. Until our own time Jewish learning was excluded from universities. Jewish young people could not undertake any aspect of Jewish studies as part of their normal education for adulthood. Now, in addition to studies in Jewish seminaries and teachers colleges, in many hundreds of colleges and universities scholars of Judaic studies, both Jewish and gentile, pursue full-time teaching and scholarship. Tens of thousands of young people in these colleges and universities take courses as part of a regular and normal liberal arts program. And in the Jewish community people treat these enormous events as if they had not taken place.

There is no bridge between the community and the campus. There is no interchange between rabbis and professors. The exception is that rabbis of the several denominations pay attention to some of the professors at the seminaries from which they got their rabbinical ordination. The exception proves the rule.

Why are things as they are, and what can be done about it?

The first cause is that scholarship seems (and often is) remote from the pressing and urgent tasks of the rabbi. Rabbis take up human crises of birth, passage through life, death. What difference does it make to them whether, in the aggregate, the Mishnah stands for one thing or another? They use what they need. For them, life is the interpretation of the text. If what scholars learn bears no clear relevance to ordinary issues of Jewish existence, it is because the scholars do not so frame their results as to address the audience at hand. They take up critical issues of Jewish existence — examples of how things have been and can be — but then fail to frame those issues in ways in which others can grasp. So what is immediate and urgent — the record of the life of the Jewish people living in accord with the same Judaism that we revere — emerges from the scholar's study as remote.

The second cause is that rabbis, for their part, have suffered a loss of position and authority. Jewish federations of philanthropies take over the leadership of the community. Important legal questions do not come to the rabbi for decision. With the advent of the professor of Judaic studies, the rabbi is no longer the only one who knows the classics of Judaism and what they mean. Indeed, with the development of congregations of better-informed, better-educated lay people, the rabbi's monopoly on serious interest in learning has fallen away.

It is difficult indeed for rabbis to know how to deal with the new sort of Jewish authority figure, represented by the university professor of Judaic studies. Rabbis cope with this figure the best way they know: They pretend the professor is not present. But she or he is present and exercises substantially more influence than rabbis pretend.

What is to be done?

First, the rabbinical associations in various places will have to recognize the existence of the professors. Further, they will have to take seriously the things that professors think are important. They must continue to learn, just as doctors and lawyers do.

Second, the professors will have to undertake to address a broad audience with the scholarly results at hand. They have to carry on a labor not only of inquiry but also of popularization. They must frame the answers they present in their scholarly work in such a way that the questions prove urgent to more than a handful of erudites. They must, therefore, themselves confess the humanity of the sources on which they labor, treating the sources, not as a set of narrow problems for technicians, but as a record of human expression and suffering and achievement.

Third, the seminaries will have to raise up a generation of rabbis who do not feel inferior to, or intimidated by, professors of Jewish learning.

Only when the rabbis respect the greatness of their own calling will they be able to take seriously the promise and partnership of others in a distinct, but contiguous calling.

An American Jewish Life:
Abraham Joshua Heschel
as a Religious Thinker

When we consider so much that is inauthentic to the
tradition of Judaism, we surely should pay attention
also to one exemplification of that tradition that is
authentic. In the world today live many Jews whose
lives are shaped by the teachings of Judaism, Jews who,
in various ways and settings, seek to live lives of holiness, to learn the Torah and to carry out and stand for
its teachings. Whether women or men, Orthodox or
Reconstructionist or Reform, these Jews testify, in
American Israel and in the State of Israel alike, to an
authentic vision. They understand that the Torah con-
veys all that we shall ever know of what it means to
be "in our image, after our likeness," that is, to be like
God. So they look for God in the Torah and in the life
that the Torah in God's name commands. And in how
they live they show us what they have found.

In our day — I speak as a third-generation American
Jew — we have known more than a few women and
men who embodied the Torah each in her or his own
distinctive manner. Let me speak of one of them, because in his own lifetime he formed the bridge from
one world to the other. In his own life he lived out the

meaning of being a Jew in America in the middle of the twentieth century.

He was Abraham Joshua Heschel, master of the Torah and teacher of the Torah. He was born in Poland in 1907, came to America in 1940, leaving Warsaw under German rule and losing most of his family in the murder of the Jews of Europe. He taught at Hebrew Union College, the Reform rabbinical seminary, in the early 1940s and in the Jewish Theological Seminary of America, the Conservative one, in the later 1940s, 1950s, and 1960s, until his death in 1971. He wrote many important works on Jewish thought and Jewish learning, covering every important classic from biblical and talmudic times to the great mystics of the eighteenth and nineteenth centuries, from philosophers such as Judah Halevi and Moses Maimonides to mystics such as the Master of the Good Name, founder of Hasidism, not to mention the great figures of nineteenth-century Jewish thought in the West. Heschel had mastered whatever there was to know. But that is not what matters. What counts is that he made it his own, and made himself over through his learning. That is why he stands for Judaism in our place and in our time.

He stands for us because he passed through the great formative experiences of our three American generations of Jews. He was an immigrant, like my grandmother. When I took her to meet him, they spoke in Yiddish, hers simple and unadorned, his poetic and unadorned. I remember hearing them talk, though I understood little of what they said, because of the

sweetness of the moment, in which my past and my
hopes for the future came together.

But he also made himself into an American, like my
father. He took an active part in Jewish community
life, lecturing wherever people wanted to hear him,
traveling endlessly.

And, like others in the third generation, he became
a critical normal figure in American life, one who
marched with Martin Luther King and in his day opposed the war in Vietnam. He stood for Judaism in
an address to the pope, spoke for world Jewry in the
crisis of 1967, rejoiced at the unification of Jerusalem,
and in his writings and his addresses spoke an authentic message of the Torah, drawing upon resources of
spirituality constantly fed and revewed through learning in the Torah and through living in the Torah.

His was the model of a life of Judaism of our day.
That is why he is important to any picture of Israel in
America. He lived it all — past and present — and
pointed the way to the future as well.

Let me explain, first and most importantly, why I
believe Heschel stands as one of the great minds of
American Judaism, a model for generations to come.
What did he try to do, and what makes his intellectual
work of lasting importance?

Heschel attempted to create a "natural theology"
for Judaism, a theology that would begin where people
actually are, in all their secularity and ignorance, and
carry them forward to Sinai. He did not define his task
in cultural or philosophical terms. That is, he did not
announce "his" position or "his" doctrine of evil. He

did not evade the theological task by announcing his "definition of the God concept," as if by defining matters, you solve a problem. What had come before him were two sorts of Judaic theologizing.

First were "scholarly" accounts of the "mind of the rabbis" and other efforts at a historical account of what certain Jews have thought in the past. These accounts exhibit many conceptual flaws, but chief among them is their unrelenting historicism. So far as the "scholarly" theologians have a theological agenda, it is to describe what those they regard as normative have had to say. The unstated corollary is that since the biblical or talmudic writers, are indeed authoritative, when we have found out what they said, we have an account of Jewish theology — what we are supposed to affirm. That is why, in Heschel's days at the Jewish Theological Seminary, the course in "theology" consisted of Louis Finkelstein's comments on *The Fathers according to Rabbi Nathan,* a Rabbinic text probably of medieval origin. By contrast Heschel was reduced to teaching elementary courses in medieval biblical exegesis to beginning students in the Seminary's Teachers Institute, a college-age program, but not allowed to teach his own theology in the Rabbinical School. To make this point clear, I suggest the analogy of a great brain surgeon being permitted to teach only comparative zoology to college sophomores. Heschel was not allowed to teach the subject of which he was the international master. The then-doyen of Talmud studies, Saul Lieberman, time and again slighted Heschel's work. It is a mark of the character of a whole genera-

tion of Jewish scholars of Judaism that Heschel tolerated the affront, both personal and intellectual. He
endured with dignity and little complaint. He went
about his work. Today those who could not bring
themselves to acknowledge his achievement are gone,
while Heschel's name and work live on. Long after
lesser scholars are forgotten. Heschel will serve as a rich
resource for Jewish thought and self-understanding.

In addition to scholarship devoted to the views of
earlier thinkers, Heschel had to contend with theology
done primarily by people trained in philosophy, particularly philosophy of religion, sometimes also social
thought. They would posit a static, concrete, one-
dimensional "thing" called Judaism. They would produce a set of propositions — "Judaism and . . ." statements — to justify and glorify Judaism. For example,
Hermann Cohen proposed that "Judaism and German
culture" constitute the highest achievement of man.
In the case of Mordecai Kaplan, knowledge of philosophy of religion in the model of John Dewey led to
abandoning the effort to think within, and through,
the classical literature of Judaic religious experience,
though Kaplan knows this literature and has given
evidence of deeply understanding it.

Other Jewish theologians had then and still have a
much less satisfactory knowledge of the classical literature to begin with. Heschel told me that Martin
Buber, for instance, received his first copy of the Talmud from Heschel on the occasion of his sixtieth
birthday; Buber thanked Heschel, saying, "I've always
wanted one." For a person to claim to be a Jewish

authority and not to know the Talmud is simply a contradiction in terms. Rosenzweig, much more celebrated than Heschel, exhibits a thin Jewish education indeed, which accounts for the external, homiletic, and evangelical quality in his writing. He had to convert to Judaism at a mature age. He knew why he affirmed, but he had to learn what. His writing, in contrast to Heschel's, exhibits little profound learning.

And then there is Heschel. What is remarkable is that he knew everything he had to know to do what he wanted to do. First, let us survey simply the subjects on which he composed interesting books: the prophets, talmudic theology of revelation, medieval philosophies (many), medieval mysticism, Hasidism, American Jewish community life, Zionism, the life of Jewish piety (Sabbath, prayer book). In point of fact, there is not a single record of Jewish religious experience, not a single moment in the unfolding of the Jewish spirit, that Heschel did not take into his own being and reshape through the crucible of his own mind and soul.

Heschel also knew the main issues of modern and contemporary philosophy of religion and followed Protestant theology. He knew and respected Tillich and Niebuhr, and they knew and respected his work. (I do not think he was equally close, in the period of his active theological work, down to the early 1960s, to any Catholic theologian, though later on, primarily on a political basis, several entered his life. I cannot find in Heschel's major writings evidence of a corresponding interest in Catholic theology.) Much of Heschel's theology constituted a post-Kantian exercise, through the medium of Judaic religious experience, in the solution of problems raised by Hume and answered by Kant.

Heschel's argument was intended, as I said, to move from natural to Judaic theology. He proposed further to demonstrate that this way led, not merely to God or generalized religiosity, but specifically to Sinai and to the Torah — yet not through a leap of faith. What philosophy of religion did not attempt was the apology for the specific claims of revealed religion. What theology did not dare to do was to join natural theology to the Torah. This is what Heschel proposed to accomplish — a brave venture.

His argument begins in this world, with that part of men and women left untouched by the critique of the Enlightenment: emotions and responses. He reaches into the inner life and looks for those elements that, present and accepted in a this-worldly framework, speak of the next world and testify to God, to the image of God impressed upon man and women. People exhibit the capacity for wonder and awe. How so? It means that not everything can be explained. The opposite of religion is taking things for granted. Wonder is a "form of thinking," an act that goes beyond knowledge.

The next stage is to take seriously the awesomeness of our very capacity to think and to respond, to wonder: "The most incomprehensible fact is the fact that we comprehend at all." From wonder comes awe, from awe, wisdom: "Awe is an intuition for the creaturely dignity of all things . . . a realization that things not only are what they are, but also stand for something absolute. Awe is a sense for the transcendence, for the reference everywhere to Him who is beyond all things." Awe precedes faith and is at its root — but itself testifies to its implication: "The ineffable is there before we form an idea of it. Yet what we affirm is the intellectual certainty that in the face of nature's grandeur and mystery we must respond with awe. What we infer from it is not a psychological state but a fundamental norm of human consciousness." This I take to be the ontological response to Kant.

This mode of argumentation is striking, for it combines two things. First, Heschel looks for natural experience accessible to everyone. But second, he claims that the experience constitutes the experiential aspect of the supernatural, of the Torah. Therefore all things are to be linked to the Hebrew Scriptures, to talmudic literature, to the holy writings of Judaism, above all to the experience of the Torah in life.

Heschel thus proposes to move from the shared experience of ordinary people to the distinctive truth of the Torah. This constitutes his primary effort to locate the foundations of natural theology and to endow them with supernatural and revelatory meaning.

When I offered this two-stage interpretation of his thinking to Heschel, he said, "Yes, you're right. But there is a third stage." I asked, "What is left out?" He said, "I won't tell you. I'm working on it now. But you're right as far as you go." Now, also, we shall never know. Clearly, his theology was an exploration of ontological issues, not epistemological ones. But where he would have gone had he lived, I cannot say.

The Christian world knew Abraham Joshua Heschel chiefly in his roles of the 1960s as holy man and politician. He was a hero to the religious sector of the left, which knew nothing of the man or the intellect, but found in Heschel an evocative symbol, a kind of authentic prophet. Heschel himself fostered that impression and enjoyed the adulation of circles responsive to his political stance, even though along with the adulation came exploitation. That his trip to Selma in the civil rights cause of the 1960s proved a disaster for the Jewish communities of Alabama and Mississippi hardly registered within his liberal and radical constituency; They were safe at home and able to enjoy a clean conscience. The Jews in the South paid a heavy price in renewed anti-Semitism.

Yet I claim this side of Heschel is ephemeral and unimportant and will soon be forgotten, when the issues of the day have changed. Heschel's good heart and good will led him, in the 1960s, to ignore the complexities of social issues and the difficulty of discovering, in political life, the entirely moral or the entirely immoral position. Heschel followed his emotions and acceded to the styles of his particular circle and political sect. It was natural. It will not matter for very long.

The Heschel who will last is in his books, and that is exactly as it should be. For Heschel spent most of his time in his study, not on the political platform or in dramatic, symbolic gestures of protest, and he was above all else a serious intellectual. None of this shows in the public Heschel, but it will endure.

Heschel's authentic existence, not his public role as a shaman for the left, focused upon his theological and scholarly enterprise. He was an exceptionally poor teacher in the classroom, but a brilliant teacher in his study. As guide, counselor, and friend, he raised up many disciples, now prominent on the right and on the left as well. In the classroom he was on the public platform, and this brought out the worst in him, a kind of second-rate academic showmanship. In his study he was fully himself, a good talker, a good listener, with wellsprings of sympathy and, above all, infinite learning.

He stood for theology in a Jewish community that did not know at the time the importance of theology. To the Jews the term *theology* is defined in the narrowest way, as "proofs for the existence of God" or, at most, discussion of the nature of God. For the many larger religious questions subsumed, for Christians, under *theology,* the Jews have different words. They speak of "Jewish thought" or "philosophy of Judaism," and very commonly of "ideology" — all of them highly secular words. Heschel insisted on calling his work theology and bravely did so in the midst of secular and highly positivistic scholars, who measured the world in terms of philological learning and thought of theology as something you do on Purim. Somehow theology is not the Torah — only philology and other safe, antiseptic subjects are the Torah.

This made Heschel's life as a theologian difficult

and sometimes bitter. He had not only to establish the legitimacy of his endeavor and to vindicate its value, but also to do it — define the work, carry it out, defend it, and change the entire context in which it is to be received. No wonder he found his political role so easy. He did not have to define the task, or create the audience, or establish the occasion. He had only to come and radiate sanctity. By contrast, his everyday task was exceedingly challenging.

If you think I exaggerate, then read the reviews of his theological books. I doubt that any other important theologian has found so little understanding of his task, let alone of his achievement of it. He was called a poet and a mystic, "un-Jewish," and dismissed as a vapid rhetorician. I cannot recall a single review (though there may have been some) that both understood what he was about and offered interesting critical comment. Either he was dismissed or he was given uncritical, often unintelligent, praise.

But Heschel should not be left in the hands of the politicians and the seekers after holy men. The story of his life is not what matters. Theologians and scholars should have no biographies. Their work is all that matters. Heschel, to be sure, was human, and therefore the great scope, ambition, and accomplishment of his work are splendid. It is the frailty of the man that makes his achievement great. His extraordinary learning was not a birthright. He worked hard. His writings were not dictated into his ear by a kindly angel. He struggled. His ideas were born in anguish and intellectual daring and courage. He was tough-minded, and his was a luminous intelligence. This should not be obscured by the public, and more easily accessible, personality.

For those within the Jewish tradition, holiness comes of learning; the luminous stands before and points toward the numinous. Heschel knew this: He spent the largest part of his life in his study because he was a rabbi and knew what a rabbi was meant to be and do. In a Jewish community by and large indifferent to Judaism and hermetically closed to learning and religiosity, led by men of wealth among the laity, or by men of an attenuated and false, manufactured charisma among the clergy, Heschel stood for something alien and authentic. To remember him is to learn what we are not, but might become — "in our image, after our likeness."

Part Five
Notes toward an Autobiography

Taking Things Apart
to See How They Work

A long time ago, when I was a boy in West Hartford, I
frame two fundamental traits that have never changed
for me. First, I had to see for myself. Second, I liked
to take things apart and to try to put them together
again to see how they worked. Whether it was a toy
car or a system of Judaism, it would always be the
same; on that my mind has never changed. As a boy I
loved learning things, finding nearly everything interesting, nearly everybody with a story to tell. That is
why I chose as my life trying to see for myself how
Judaism worked, learning about nearly everything in
the quest for that one goal; on that my mind has never
changed. I want to see how diverse groups of Jews
worked out the way of life and the world view that
framed their world. I want to know what it is about
us as human beings that we learn from them — how,
in the mirror of their world, we see a small detail of
ourselves, of us as humanity, as we are in God's likeness, in God's image. On that my mind will never
change: We are in the likeness, we are in the image.

But on most other things, as in the nature of things,
my mind changes every day, and why not? For to re-
flect and reconsider is a mark of learning and growth,

a measure of curiosity and intellectual capacity. For us who spend our lines as teachers and learners in the realm of religion in the here and now, to reach a firm and final "position" means to die, to stop our quest. For our subject lives, changes, grows. If both in books and in the faces of the day we search for the record of God's image and God's likeness, then we can never finally master all the data or reach a firm conviction, short of knowing everything about everything and understanding it all, once for all.

I will be forgiven, therefore, if in the small and remote corner of the world in which I conduct my quest for what it means to be a human being, I seek, and find, new understanding from day to day. To say how my mind has changed is to catalog all that I have learned, specifying what is worth remembering or forgetting. My career, that is, my education in the study of Judaism, goes back to 1954, when I became a beginning student at the Jewish Theological Seminary of America. Happily for oratorical purposes, my career divides into three periods, each of a decade: the historical, the literary, and the cultural. I work on the Talmud and related literature. In my historical period, into the 1960s, I wanted to know what happened in the *time* of the Talmud. In my literary period, into the 1970s, I wanted to know what happened in the *pages* of the Talmud. In my cultural period, into the 1980s, I wanted to know what happened because of what is *said* in the Talmud.

So for a decade I worked on the Talmud and related writings as a historical source, for another decade I worked on the Talmud as a literary problem, and in the present period I work on the Talmud as a statement of culture, as an artifact of human expression, as a solution to someone's problem. For thirty years my mind remained fixed on the view that we have in hand, first, the record of a remarkable experiment in being human, hence a historical record, and, second, a complex and subtle experiment in recording, through *how* things are said as much as through what is said, the lessons people have learned from their experiment, hence, a literary monument. But, third and most important, there is something still more immediate. For what makes the Talmud and related literature not only interesting but also important for contemporary discourse on the human situation is not its historical facts or literary presence. If only Jews searching for their own heritage studied the Talmud as a work of law and theology, history and literature, or a labor of faith and devotion to God's word, the rest of humanity would lose out on a small but valued part of the treasury of human experience. It is the testimony of the Talmud and related literature on a common human problem that we then should press.

Let me explain. When we consider the human situation of those Jews whose history and literature, whose law and theology, we have at hand, we understand the critical importance of that third dimension, that third decade — the 1980s — of my own life as a scholar, the dimension of the Talmud as a social construct, as a statement, beyond itself and its details, of a transcendent, larger whole. But who can hear it all, and all at once? The genius of a composer is to draw together many voices and enable them not only to speak all at once, which is mere cacophony, but also to speak simultaneously and yet intelligibly and harmoniously, which is music, opera, for instance. What composer can draw together so vast a literature, so diverse a set of themes and motifs, and form the whole into a whole? That, phrased in the language of music we all share, is the problem of a scholar's labor. Is it any wonder that, as I said at the outset, my mind should change and change and change? But if I am to be judged, as we all must be judged if we propose to do things with our lives, then let me be condemned if I waste my opportunities, or let me be exonerated if I have freely exercised my powers of imagination and used my strength to grasp the whole and hold it all in balance, if I have shown imagination and capacity.

Let me then spell out this matter of imagination. What is wrong with reading the Talmud and related literature as only a historical record, as only a literary monument? And what is right about listening for its statement of culture and seeing it as an artifact of humanity faced with a particular problem? I want to ask you to think not about ancient Israel in the aftermath of a catastrophe of defeat, ancient Israel no longer in control of its land and of its life, ancient Israel facing a world less hospitable than any it had ever known. Rather I want to speak of Wales after Edward, Scotland after 1745, and Ireland after Cromwell, after England. I swim every day with a sculptor of Canadian-Scottish origin. He explained to me why the Scots in Canada — at least, his family — will not plant sweet william in their gardens and wear a black armband on the sixteenth of April. After nearly two and a half centuries and two nations later, the Scots remain defeated, beleaguered, out of kilter. Some people here may have followed the "Masterpiece Theater" performance of "To Serve Them All Our Days," and may recall that the Welsh hero, in an English public school, tells the headmaster that he cannot make it in England because he is "of the wrong nationality," and tells his girlfriend that the castles on the English-Welsh border are there to keep out "his" ancestors. The Welsh have not had their own nation for nearly seven centuries. But in their own mind they are Israel beyond catastrophe. And who needs to be reminded of the suffering of the Irish, whose history rivals that of us Jews for its pathos — its resentment and its long-nursed righteous grievance. I could not watch the end of the TV history of Ireland, any more than I could watch TV portrayals of the murder of the Jews of Europe. I cannot distinguish among those events that fall into the classification of "holocaust," to use the prevailing linguistic symbol. This digression carries us far from biblical and related studies, but it is important in explaining why I see the Talmud and related literature as a worthy object of today's imagination. It is worth trying to grasp the whole and hold it all in balance, because only in that way shall we be able to see the humanity in the circumstance preserved in those difficult and contentious writings, and only in that way shall we gain access to that distinctive version of a human experience common to us all. I mean defeat, disappointment, resentment, but also renewal and sanctification.

That is why, to state matters briefly, I changed my mind about the value of historical inquiry by itself, and rejected the self-evidence of the worth of literary inquiry by itself. But I affirm them both in a larger search for meaning, for insight resting upon learning. We have to know what in fact happened, what came first and what took place next. The sources at hand, nevertheless, will stand in judgment of our work and find it insufficient, if that is all we want to ask them. For they have *more* to tell us. But as I think most of us now realize, they also have much *less* to tell us. The Talmud and related literature do not come to us from the hand of trained reporters, with tape recorders and video cameras, and people have to read these sources in the same critical spirit that guides their reading of the Hebrew Scripture and the New Testament and much else. The first ten years of my life, marked by the *Life of Yohanan ben Zakkai* and the *History of the Jews in Babylonia,* defined a long struggle to emerge from fundamentalist reading of Rabbinic tales and stories, on the one side, and fundamentalist description of the life and culture of the Jews of that age, on the other.

I thought that if we could show *how* the sources work, we could gain access to their historical records. That is why, in the next ten years, I took up problems of literary criticism, involving, in particular, the familiar and routine methods of form analysis, redaction criticism, dissection and reconstruction — in all, the methods of an acerbic and cool encounter. That decade at hand — the 1970s — marked the transition that is critical to the future. I began the literary work with an interest in problems of a historical character, which I proposed to investigate through a critical reading of the diverse sources generally alleged to give information about those problems. My three studies of this period involved a first-century rabbi — Yohanan ben Zakkai revisited — then the Pharisees before A.D. 70, and, finally, a critical figure in the age of reconstruction after the destruction of the Temple in A.D. 70, Eliezer ben Hyrcanus. In all three cases I wanted to read the sources critically, as they had not been read, essentially in order to produce answers to historical questions, such as had been answered many times before. The method was new to its field (but only to that field). But the program was old and familiar. That was the first half of the decade, from the late 1960s to the middle 1970s. But, alas, minds change. I continued the literary work with an interest in problems of a cultural, anthropological character.

Throughout the work at hand — under way for fifteen years, from 1960 to 1975 — I faced the growing sense that everything I was doing was beside the point of the sources. By the mid-1970s, I realized that the questions were mine, but *not* theirs. My Orthodox Jewish friends always had told me this, since they thought history irrelevant (they called it the story of what a rabbi had for lunch, not the story of what he stood for). They thought critical literary methods either heretical or old hat (I never could tell which). But the questions of my Orthodox Jewish friends were those *of* the text. They asked little of interest to our own day. What I needed to find were questions that would be my questions as well as questions congruent with the answers that the *texts* provided in their ancient day. To move forward, in the same decade, in the late 1970s, I shifted my program. I wanted still to read the sources critically as literature, and I wanted still to come up with historical answers, a picture of how things were, not merely how the text portrays them. But what questions, what answers? I determined to ask the texts to tell me what *they* wanted to discuss, rather than what interested me. That meant to ask the Mishnah to be the Mishnah, the Tosefta, its supplement, to speak in *its* terms and along its own lines, so too the two Talmuds and the more important collections of exegeses of Scripture (midrashim).

The present decade, the 1980s, for me is the age in which I am trying to describe the documents one by one *but each one whole.* I have thus far addressed the Mishnah as a whole and in its components, in my *Judaism: The Evidence of the Mishnah* (1981), in the same exercise I deal also with the Tosefta. I have completed my first soundings in the Talmud of the Land of Israel, with the results in the paired works of volume 35 of *The Talmud of the Land of Israel. Introduction: Taxonomy* and *Judaism in Society: The Evidence of the Yerushalmi.* And I have dealt at some length with one collection of scriptural exegeses and asked how the framers of that collection appear to have thought they made a cogent and intelligible statement. This work is in *Judaism and Scripture: The Evidence of Leviticus Rabbah.* My present work takes up the same issues for the Babylonian Talmud. Essentially, therefore, I have reached the point that, in my childhood, I would reach when I had taken the toy car apart and laid out all its bits and pieces.

No one will be surprised to know that it is harder to put things together than it is to take them apart. In three works I have tried to follow the familiar path of working on a particular problem according to the route dictated by the character of the documents. Exploiting the earlier results of the description of documents one by one, and each one whole, I asked about the three fundamental questions of description of any religious system: revelation and canon, teleology and eschatology, and generative symbol. The works that have come out are *Midrash in Context: Exegesis in Formative Judaism, Messiah in Context: Israel's History and Destiny in Formative Judaism,* and *Torah: From Scroll to Symbol in Formative Judaism.* Clearly the third decade is nearly over.

What lies before me is that ultimate question of childhood: How does it really work? Once, as I said, we have taken the car apart and seen how it is made up, can we put it together again? Just where and why and how did the system work, specifically, that system of Judaism created by the ancient rabbis and attested in their writings? To state matters somewhat differently, we know that the documents at hand fall into a single context, namely, that of the ancient rabbis. We also know that they come in a single classification, namely (for ancient times), (A) Jewish and (B) rabbinical writings. We know, more importantly, that the ancient documents are represented in various ways as being connected to one another. They not only fit together in one classification but also join together with one or another *within* that classification. The real question before us is not one of classification or connectedness, therefore, but rather one of continuity. Are these texts continuous, and if so, what moves from one to the next and how does the movement take place? How do the diverse documents constitute one "Judaism"? True, in the eye of faith all of the documents at hand form a single statement, one of "Judaism," or, in the language of the faith, of "Torah." But that conviction forms a datum of the contemporary faith, not an analytical or categorical postulate. No one present thinks otherwise, unless you also regard the conviction that there is one holy Catholic church, a single Christianity, a "church that is one in Christ" — profound Christian affirmations — as serviceable descriptions of the this-worldly history and character of Christian churches. So too with "Judaism" or "Torah."

Readers unfamiliar with the range of Jewish learning will wonder why I claim that the work "begins" at this point. Has not the Talmud been studied for fifteen centuries? Indeed it has, but not in this way and not for this purpose. Is the Talmud not studied elsewhere than in America? In truth it is, but not in the broad, humanistic and unpolemical context found in America. The claim of this book, that America serves as a felicitous and appropriate home for Israel, as much as any country in the entire history of Israel, the Jewish people, and as much as the State of Israel today, rests in the end upon the judgment offered here. In my view Jewish learning, a barometer and indicator of the health of the Jewish people, Israel, flourishes in America in fresh and important ways. The character of the scholarly program I have outlined here typifies work done by many others in this country and Canada, and by few others anywhere else. Israeli scholarship is different from ours, totally out of sympathy with ours, and unable to comprehend the issues that in general attract humanistic scholars to the classical sources of diverse cultural and religious traditions, including, for one example only, Judaism. In America, Jewish learning enjoys a new beginning. So I say, let the work begin.

14

My Generation:
The Third

One of my sons, when he wants to know how things were when I was his age, asks, "What were things like when you were alive?" Just as the young cannot imagine that their parents know about sex, so they cannot comprehend that their parents are alive in the same way in which the young are alive. They may have a point.

My generation — the third generation of American Jewry, now in its fifties and sixties — cared and dreamed and worried, and is now finished. Why? Because, by and large, the things we wanted to make happen have happened, and the young see us as finished.

I grew up in West Hartford, Connecticut, a suburb of Hartford, when only a few Jews lived there. I remember, about being Jewish, only two things: First, I thought it was something to do only in private, and, second, I wondered whether it would be done at all for very much longer.

I came, please understand, from a very Jewish — though not at all Judaic — family, so I was one of those who cared about being Jewish. I was, for example, the only one in my group who voted for Roosevelt in 1944 (as a sixth grader). And I was the only one in my group who knew that something of great importance was happening in 1948. Most of the Jewish kids I knew were not interested in being Jewish and did a good job of adapting their appearance and behavior to match their lack of interest. My mother, a matriarch of the second generation, was proud of not having been born in "Europe," which was less a place than a state of mind. (In our house, everything vulgar and tasteless was "European.") She called me Jackie, until my voice deepened, and then she called me Jack. But it was only when I turned twenty-one and applied for my first passport that I discovered that my name, my only name, the name bestowed upon me at birth and hidden from me for more than two decades, was not Jackie, was not Jack, was, in fact, Jacob.

Those few of us who thought about being Jewish, who were part of the generation that was too young for the Second World War, too old for Vietnam, excused from Korea by virtue of student deferments, that seemed stuck in the cracks between great historical events, we worried about the Jewish future. We knew how few we were, and we knew how different we were from our grandparents, how far removed from the manifest wellsprings of faith and commitment and culture, and we could not imagine what a Jewish future might be built upon, from what new springs it would draw its strength.

Specifically, we could not know and did not guess that most of our friends, the ones who did not know and did not care, the ones who were busy "waspifying" themselves, would one day marry Jews and join

synagogues and temples and choose to live near other
Jews and care about Israel — in short, that they would
want to be Jews.

The mystery of the third generation is this: Jewish
but not too Jewish. Not so Jewish that you stop being
an American. We knew about that from our grandparents, who had remained too European ever to become Americans. Our parents tried to overcome the
sense of being alien, and succeeded. They became undifferentiated Americans, to everyone except themselves. And we, in our turn, became for a time what
our parents wanted us to be — undifferentiated Americans, to everyone, ourselves included.

Those of us who knew from early on that the Jews
were supposed to last, who wanted the Jewish connection to survive, were, as I have said, few in number.
I recall that one day, when I was in the ninth grade,
I was walking along Farmington Avenue when a terrible
thought occurred to me. A time would come, I realized,
when the rabbi of our (Reform) temple would be dead,
and my father, too, would die. And then I would be
the last Jew on earth — or, at least, on Farmington
Avenue in West Hartford. That was the day I decided
to become a rabbi, a decision I promptly shared with
the whole world. My parents were puzzled. Years later,
it is what those who knew me then most remember:
"He was the one who wanted to become a rabbi!"

What I really wanted to be and to become, of course,
was a Jew. But I must have sensed that for our generation, being Jewish would require a special kind of
effort and commitment. It had to become a vocation,

because, left to flourish in a less explicit environment, it would not flourish at all. Since there was no longer a sustaining environment, it would wither. One had to set out to discover Judaism and self-consciously to make a Jew of oneself, because we had neither encountered it nor been invited, nor, perhaps, even permitted, to encounter it as we grew up.

We wanted most to be part of a community that would share our concern for "being Jewish," whatever that might mean. In our day, that meant finding others who shared that most peculiar wish — in seminaries, in youth movements, in a few other scattered places. And when we found those places, we used them to try to expand the Jewish possibility, to make the entire community a congenial place for our Jewish aspirations.

And that is why the work of my generation is now over. We won the fight.

Think about it: If there had been an "organized Jewish community" back when I was growing up, it was so remote that we never heard about it. In towns such as ours, federations did not yet exist or, if they did, scarcely thought of themselves as anything more than welfare agencies for the distressed. The Jewish community center was inaccessible, had no program that I can remember hearing of. There were few camps of Jewish content (though I went to a camp where everyone was Jewish), no youth movements to speak of (except for misfits). I never knew about the *Shabbat;* I never saw a sukkah. I remember how shocked I was, when I went to Oxford, to meet young Jews

of intellectual distinction who knew the grace after
meals — yes, the *birkat hamazon* — and said it. When
I was at Harvard, the few observant Jews, almost all
the sons of rabbis, were curiosities.

A Jewish community? To be built from what? Where
were the people; where were the models? That is what
we wanted to know, and there was no answer save as
we ourselves, we few, were ready to be the people, to
provide the models.

But to make that work, to make it last, to make it
possible for our children to step easily into a living
community, we had to develop a public agenda as
well. We had to force the Jewish community to resolve its own ambivalence so that, I suppose, we could
resolve ours. Either become Jewish, really Jewish,
whatever that might come to mean, be made to mean,
or stop bothering about it, stop insisting on the difference, stop insisting even on survival.

Accordingly, we approached the community back
in the late 1940s and early 1950s with a peculiar set
of demands. I remember, for instance, my earliest
writings on the budgets of Jewish federations, published in my father's newspaper (the *Connecticut
Jewish Ledger,* which we subsequently sold). I ana-
lyzed the budgets of the federation from year to year,
and wondered in print what was Jewish about them
or it. Later on, our group — for we few became a kind
of group — went on to ask what was Jewish about
Jewish community centers, and again, we found remarkably few answers. We wanted more attention to
be paid to the State of Israel than was the norm back

then, before the earthquakes and revolutions that transfixed the entire community. Ah, there was so much that we wanted!

And we got it. We got it all.

We were right to want it; we were right to get it. For the third generation, for the generation that married Jewish but did not know why, that wanted Jewish but did not know how, we provided the structure of organizations and the intellectual underpinnings that today serve as the foundation of organized Jewry in this country. My own three "projects" were the reform of federations, the formation of *havurot* (small groups formed for religious encounter), and the development of Jewish studies in universities. The federations have now become principle vehicles of Jewish expression and continuity; *havurot* multiply and are fruitful; and Jewish studies in universities, both quantitatively and qualitatively, have achieved distinction.

But what we wanted and needed and achieved, we wanted and needed for ourselves, not for those to come. What we accomplished was in response to our own agenda, an agenda that grew out of our own distinctive experience as the third generation. The world of our children is paradoxically different from our own. For them, being Jewish is much less a given, a fixed condition, than it was for us, just as it was less a given for us than it had been for our parents, less for our parents than for our grandparents. But at the same time, the *crafting* of Jewish lives, of a Jewish life, is no longer the laborious, idiosyncratic effort it was for us. Young Jews today have available to them a Jewish education far richer than we had. Schools, summer camps, youth programs, and, of course, the State of Israel — these form a set of educational resources that is rich beyond anything we dreamed of. As well as an intermarriage rate larger than we imagined we could bear. As well as a growing number of converts to Judaism. Paradoxes all the time.

These are paradoxes that will not be resolved until the fourth generation matures. I am inclined to be hopeful, for that is my nature, but I am also mindful of Arthur Hertzberg's warning: "There is more passion for Jerusalem and more loyalty to Judaism in the American Jewish community today than we shall have in a decade, *if we do not do some radical things now.*"

I agree with Hertzberg, but I also think that we, who are no longer alive, are not the ones to do what now wants doing or even to say very much about what that might be. It is for the living to name what needs to be done and to do it, because the work of the next age, whatever it is, will have to respond to the agenda of a generation that was framed by different experiences from our own and is defined by different needs. I do not see that there is much for "the organized Jewish community" to do these days except not to block or to blight what still-unheard-of-names will soon be proposing, perhaps even demanding.

So here I am, about to pass the torch. But first a word of advice, from the rocking chair to the runner.

Don't make the mistakes that I, or others like me, made.

We all were drawn into the value system of the organized community as it existed in our day. We took seriously what we were not and apologized for what we were. We pretended to think, and some of us even came to think, that there is something more important than ideas. We who spend our lives in classrooms and in libraries, in studies, pulpits, editorial offices, the places where intellectuals do their work, learned a whole new vocabulary, chose to play on alien turf. We were intellectuals out to reshape the world we loved, the Jewish world, but we neglected our own gifts of intellect and heart, our own vocabulary. Instead, we raised issues of material and mass, issues to which we had nothing special to contribute.

What, after all, were the points of the reforms we proposed and effected? They had to do with the spending of money, the building of institutions, the ordering of priorities. We wanted the federations to spend their money on consequential things, Jewish things. So they did.

And now we have learned that money is not the answer.

We wanted the synagogues to organize themselves in ways that related to the individual and his needs, in this time, in this place, to permit the formation of groups where people would not feel lost. So they did.

And now we have learned that organizing an institution in one way rather than in another is not the answer.

We wanted the community to focus its attention on the great cultural resources represented by the State of Israel, to pay attention, as it had not adequately

done in the 1940s and 1950s, to the political requirements of Zionism. So it did.

And now we have learned that our salvation does
not lie in the East.

It is important to remember that we were not frustrated in the pursuit of our goals. Our disappointments
derive from other sources, not from our failure, but
from our success.

How is it that we were so very successful? Chiefly,
we came to the community with what it already was
coming to know. We were just a bit early on the scene.
Even without us, the passionate reformers of the
1950s and 1960s, what we like to think we had a hand
in making happen would have happened anyway.
Some things might have taken a bit longer, but they
would have happened. The community was in the
hands of practical and effective and intelligent people,
both lay and professional. They had as much good will
as we and as much constructive purpose. They, too,
understood what needed to be done, and they did it.
They drew on what they had: money and organizational skill.

What we should have known all along, but are only
now coming to see, is that neither money nor organization can secure our future. And when we chose to
play on alien turf, we added only another layer of
veneer to the House of Israel in America, a house that
still has no solid foundation.

I am not saying that we were wrong to make the
choices that we made. I am saying only that those
choices are no longer the choices that need making,

and it is disheartening to encounter so many, third and fourth generation alike, who persist in fighting yesterday's wars. Our victory in those wars makes possible a new war. And to win that war, too, intellectuals will have to hold to the end.

The new war is to shape an idea, not a shared consensus, but a consensus worth sharing. There is simply no corpus of intellectually consequential ideas about what it means to be a Jew, here and now, in this time and in this place, to which Jewry today has access. The ideas the rabbis preach must come from somewhere; the policies expressed in federation meetings have to begin with someone. If theology and ideology for contemporary Jewry were merely what people pretend — a conventional apologetic, a ritual of excuses — it might not matter. But ideas do move people; without ideas, people will not move. They will merely twitch, pretending life.

What people think really matters. It is embarrassing to have to write these words. Yet the words are no longer obvious. They are not obvious to the formers and shapers of Jewry because we who formed the corpus of ideas, of theology and ideology, over the last thirty years behaved as if people were secondary, and actions primary. As perhaps they were — for a time. We did not invite the shapers and movers to our turf — we eagerly invaded theirs. We led them to believe that in their distance from the life of the Jewish intellect, from Jewish ideas, in their remove from the soul of Judaism, they could and should do whatever would secure a worthy Jewish present and a viable vision of a Jewish future. They looked to us for ideas. And we talked to them of money and how to spend it.

They had power, and we imagined ourselves impotent. So when they invited us to join them, that is exactly what we did, forgetting that if all we had to offer was a pale imitation of the resources they already had, they would not have wanted us or needed to invite us. They did not know how to ask the question, and we did not hear the question they did not ask, the only question we might have been able to answer with some authority. We were too enamored with the trappings. So we lost our voice; we answered other questions, questions whose answers were already known, questions that mattered but that did not require us to answer them. We behaved like directors of agencies: asked for money, competed for money. And offered nothing of what we knew. Pretended to be sophisticated. Lost our nerve, our sense of self.

Ideas come first. Vision takes precedence. The educated heart is what creates and shapes our energies to act. Did not the State of Israel begin in the minds of dissatisfied intellectuals? Was it not born as an idea? Was it not shaped by first-class minds? Long before there was a Jewish state, there was the idea of a Jewish state, and there would never have been a Jewish state without that idea. An idea: mostly talk — but what a conversation, and what an impact!

So it is with the great movements of every age. They start in our minds, not in our bellies (*pace* the communists and the federations alike), not in our bank accounts. And when intellectuals are responsible for events, it is because they develop ideas that are compelling, not because they aspire to positions of power. The seductive attraction of high office subverts the far greater power that intellectuals who do not deny themselves might exercise.

So there is the advice. Do not be other than what. you are. In this context, let those with ideas remain true to their hearts, their minds, their intellects. We are a people to whom a book is an event, a rare insight, an occasion for celebration. Let me refer back to Abraham Heschel, who in the late 1950s put forth an intellectual heritage still not adequately interpreted or understood. His monumental intellectual achievements of that period received no hearing either then or later. As I said earlier, it was during the 1960s that he became a public figure and gained a vast and impressive hearing — but that was not for his distinctive intellectual contribution. I cannot blame him, but I think we would be better off today had he pursued, in his last years, those lines of thought and modes of reflection that in a few brief years yielded *Man Is Not Alone* and *God in Search of Man.* Heschel's public power was vastly greater in the 1960s than it had been in the 1950s. But it was a different kind of power, and it yielded different products, and all of them have now evaporated. He represents the curious ambiguities of the third generation, its risky compromise.

The plain fact is that the future of American Jewry will not be decided by the synagogues, the federations, the centers, the day schools, the hospitals, the American Jewish Committees, and the Anti-Defamation

Leagues. Nor will it be settled by raising another billion dollars for the State of Israel, nor even a billion
dollars for Jewish education and culture. The future
of American Jewry will be decided, for better or worse,
by the ideas that American Jews have and come to
have about their future. It will be settled by what the
fourth generation manages to achieve by way of a set
of ideas. We of the third generation built a building,
and that was important to do. It is time now to place
a foundation under that building. That has yet to be
done. And that foundation does not take dollars. It
takes words, and ideas.

Index

203

Jacob Neusner is co-director of the Program in Judaic Studies at Brown University, where he has taught for the past seventeen years. He has authored over one hundred books on Jewish history and theology.